BAD HOMBRES

HOW HISPANICS WILL SAVE AMERICA

STEVE CORTES

Published by Bombardier Books
An Imprint of Post Hill Press
ISBN: 978-1-63758-939-7
ISBN (eBook): 978-1-63758-940-3

Bad Hombres:
How Hispanics Will Save America

Cover Design by Jim Villaflores
Cover Photo by Andre Dantzler

This is a work of nonfiction. All people, locations, events, and situations are portrayed to the best of the author's memory.

Post Hill Press
New York • Nashville
posthillpress.com

Published in the United States of America
1 2 3 4 5 6 7 8 9 10

TABLE OF CONTENTS

INTRO PART ONE

Hispanics are going to save America.

In fact, *only* "bad hombres" can save America from our garbage elites.

The phrase "bad hombres" entered the American lexicon for most non-Spanish speakers during the 2016 presidential campaign. After his famous escalator descent in the Trump Tower, TV celebrity, business mogul, and presidential candidate Donald Trump announced he would be running for president. In his campaign, he warned about the many dangers of America's weak borders, especially how they allow rebels and criminals, dubbed "bad hombres," to enter America with ill intent.

Fast forward five years later, and this phrase was still stuck in my head. In conservative circles, the title had been adopted as a tongue-in-cheek compliment to Hispanics in the America First movement, especially Latino men who are often on the frontline ramparts of the battle to reclaim our country.

This newly coined understanding of "bad hombres" came to mind as I read the names of Hispanic US Marines who died in 2021. As a cable news prime time host, I was broadcasting about the awful consequences of Joe Biden's botched, disastrous withdrawal from Afghanistan.

America needed to leave Afghanistan. Though the war had already slouched into a quagmire many years prior, the Washington War Machine predictably succeeded in prolonging a pointless foreign intervention for nearly a generation. This massive mistake by the DC foreign policy establishment led to trillions of borrowed dollars being wasted on the war on terror and far too many US families losing loved ones. For all those tragically killed, many more came home badly wounded, either physically or psychologically.

The avoidable loss of life during the ill-planned withdrawal provided an almost fitting ending to this twenty-year establishment boondoggle. Thirteen brave American servicemen were killed by a terrorist attack at the Abbey Gate of the Kabul International Airport.

Without diving into the policy errors that led to this preventable loss of American life, the composition of the dead US heroes was striking. Of the eleven marines who offered the ultimate sacrifice for America, five of them were Hispanic with Latin names.[1] Hispanics grow in numbers every year in America—a combination of both immigration rates and a higher birth rate than other ethnicities—leading them to constitute 18 percent of the total US

1 Andrea Scott, "Here are the names of the 13 U.S. service members killed in Afghanistan attack" (*Marine Corps Times,* August 28, 2021), https://www.marinecorpstimes.com/news/your-marine-corps/2021/08/28/here-are-the-names-of-the-13-service-members-who-died-in-afghanistan-attack/

population.[2] Yet they comprised nearly half of the brave Marines who died for America on that fateful day in August 2021.

Was this simply an anomaly?

Once I studied the issue and spoke to several marines, both active duty and veterans, I learned about the crucial role Hispanics play in their beloved Corps. Many of its best rifle companies, for example, are dominated by tough, young, bad hombre Hispanics. Because of their bravery, Hispanic military volunteers across the services are often sent into some of most difficult and dangerous missions possible in defense of the country they love.

Though many of these heroes hail from families that are only recently American, they still embrace a love of their newfound "patria"—their homeland. Such affection is now sadly unusual among most credentialed Americans of the established ruling class, even though their ancestral lines may trace back to the colonial days of America.

As I read those names and learned about the impressive young lives of these bad hombres and one proud female Latina, it dawned on me that Hispanics must save this country. Even more, Hispanics represent the only hope to save America.

These bad hombres will not be saving America from foreign adversaries—though those threats are real, especially from China. But this vanguard of God-fearing, flag-waving, family-embracing bad hombres will primarily be saving America from a corrupt garbage elite that has pushed this country to the brink of ruin.

---

2 Bill Wiatrowski, "Expanded data for detailed Hispanic or Latino groups now available" (US Bureau of Labor Statistics, October 6, 2023), https://www.bls.gov/blog/2023/expanded-data-for-detailed-hispanic-or-latino-groups-now-available.htm#:~:text=Hispanics%20accounted%20for%2017.8%20percent,Spanish%20in%20the%20survey%20process

As such, when America looks for saviors, those who presently occupy positions of power will prove unwilling and unable to lead a national renewal. Most of them happen to be white men, and most of them have either acquiesced or surrendered to the woke leftist mob that operates in cahoots with the oligarchy. Others have been too marginalized in post-pandemic America to be effective in reclaiming our republic and saving our country.

Now, does America really need saving? Tragically, yes. The evidence abounds that America slides into a state of depressed anxiety. For example, a recent Wall Street Journal poll asked citizens if their children will be better off than they are. A stunning 78 percent said no, by far the worst mark ever in a survey that extends back over three decades.[3]

Similarly, polling of the swing states from my nonprofit political advocacy firm, League of American Workers, reveals a marked decline of confidence in the American Dream. For example, in the key battleground state of Arizona, only 18 percent of voters said that the American Dream is still attainable.[4] Fewer than one in five!

In addition to polling, nearly every important grassroots metric further validates this pervasive sentiment. For example, suicide rates soar, especially among the young. Trends toward economic inequality worsen dramatically, and indebtedness deepens at both the personal and national levels. Substance abuse climbs, and overall health deteriorates. Take a trip to a typical Walmart

---

[3] Janet Adamy, "Most Americans Doubt Their Children Will Be Better Off, WSJ-NORC Poll Finds" (*The Wall Street Journal*, March 24, 2023), https://www.wsj.com/articles/most-americans-doubt-their-children-will-be-better-off-wsj-norc-poll-finds-35500ba8

[4] Jon McHenry and Dan Judy, "Key Findings from Survey of Arizona Likely Voters" (*North Star Opinion Research*, November 15, 2023), https://www.amworkers.com/news

and these truths become obvious. Our society struggles. We are less healthy, less optimistic, and far less patriotic.

But rather than simply curse the darkness, we must, as the Good Book says, light a candle. We must ascertain the path up and out from this morass, and then do everything possible to facilitate a national rebirth. Politics is critical to national renewal, though it is certainly not the only necessary element.

In this book, I will detail evidence and data that strongly point to Hispanics leading this American renaissance—a movement that will create positive change in national culture, demography, economy, and confidence.

INTRO PART TWO

As the largest minority group in America, Hispanics stand uniquely capable of leading a rebirth of this great, but failing, republic. In fact, unless Hispanics lead this charge, America is destined for further protracted decline.

Why has America wandered upon such a dismal trajectory, necessitating a national rebirth, and why does this burden fall upon Hispanics?

To the second question, the simple answer is that only Hispanics have the culture, ethics, faith, and scale to save this floundering nation. In contrast, other Americans are too conflicted and compromised for this great task.

Though the majority of America is still Anglo, ruling-class Caucasians in the United States have been more than happy to succumb to a pervasive, toxic white guilt for decades. In fact, the most connected and corrupted crony establishment white actors have powerfully utilized anti-white sentiment and unjust white guilt for their personal aggrandizement.

White Americans, at least those who comprise the credentialed ruling class in America, now almost all fit into two categories: the collaborators or the ostracized. The first group gladly plays ball with the secular humanist Left, mainly for personal power, wealth, and prestige. Some of these white managerial class people of influence have actually convinced themselves that America is some inherently bigoted creation—one deserving of scorn.

Most of these who actually believe the leftist drivel subscribe to ahistorical and illogical views of America. They are, paradoxically, the most highly "educated" people in our nation. In today's upside-down society, the supposedly smarter a person is, the dumber they actually are in real life. Simply reflect, for example, upon the COVID-19 panic. The educated, advanced, degree-holding communities acted the most hysterically, and they behaved in manners totally inconsistent with science or logic. Blue collar—especially Hispanic—communities acted far more rationally.

But I strongly suspect that most of the collaborators among the white managerial class know the truth. They subscribe to the dominant ruling-class narratives about America, but they know, deep down, that the prevailing ethos of the Left rests on totally flawed thinking and a tyrannical, communistic thirst for power. But these cowards play ball with the Left anyway. Why? For money and status.

They cringe internally, but they will not jeopardize their corner office at the multinational by objecting to indoctrination session "training" courses. These classes are inflicted upon millions of American workers. These laborers, often hardworking hourly employees, are patronized and informed they have "white privilege"—even though they struggle to afford the necessities of life amid the economic carnage of Bidenomics.

These same credentialed, white managerial class eunuchs simply stay quiet as they watch sports on TV and every other commercial showcases a multi-racial, homosexual couple. As parents, they are too scared to confront the supposedly prestigious local school, whether public or private, when it inflicts a curriculum upon children that prepares them to be pampered victims rather than strong warriors, builders, and caregivers for a great nation.

Consider the example of white female academic Robin DiAngelo who wrote the offensive and bigoted screed, *White Fragility*. Dr. DiAngelo parlayed her University of Washington PhD in sociology into a hugely influential and massively lucrative career by making whites feel terrible about themselves. As a tenured professor, she pontificated from an ivory tower about supposed "privilege," which would sure be news to tens of millions of white Americans who struggle to make ends meet and afford the basic necessities of life.

Because of DiAngelo's success as a media darling of the corrupt corporate press, she forged a lucrative side hustle as an "educator" on all matters regarding race, sought after by corporations and other intimidated organizations. In reality, many societal leaders—from big business CEOs to college presidents—do not really subscribe to the ludicrous notion that America is, in 2024, a systemically racist country. Nonetheless, they comply with absurd propaganda efforts and spew out toxic, anti-white insults at customers and employees anyway.

Why?

Because such efforts provide cover. They construct a sort of invincibility shield to protect against crazed leftists, whether it be the activist class or, even worse, government apparatchiks wielding the almighty power of the state. Playing along with race-baiting storytelling with mouthpieces like DiAngelo provides modern American organizations with today's equivalent of the Passover protections of the Old Testament. "Nothing to see here, folks. At XYZ Corporation, we too know that white people suck, and everything the company has built is effectively stolen from the simple, yet noble, natives who lived here long before any evil palefaces showed up."

But many companies and white societal leaders go way beyond engaging with the mere protection racket. Others, like Larry Fink of the financial behemoth BlackRock, fully exploit these leftist ideologies for massive profit.

Fink is perhaps the most powerful man in America that almost nobody knows anything about. In fact, he may very well manage your money. Even if Fink is not directly investing your retirement funds, he almost surely is indirectly placing your taxpayer resources as he manages public monies at all levels of government.

Like DiAngleo, Fink publicly takes a stance as a strident, professional apologist; his "crime" is being a white heterosexual male who frequently uses fossil fuels. Because BlackRock owns substantial stakes in almost every major company in America, Fink's influence extends throughout society. The other conglomerate asset management firms—the Vanguard and State Street components of Big Money—also play similar games.

Because the garbage elites of the United States have almost totally sold out to leftist insanity, and because the ruling class is still comprised overwhelmingly of white Americans, the entire demographic of white citizens becomes largely neutered as a societal force for reform. In other words, whites on their own have no forcefield protection. By the absurd norms and mores of America since Obama and George Floyd, the only way for Caucasians to gain equal status in our culture, media, big business, and academia is to completely sell out and trash whites!

There are, of course, millions of sensible white Americans who are not collaborators and refuse to surrender to these ridiculous lies of the Left. These are the patriots who know US history and proudly wave the flag of a nation that has always, until recent years, made progress toward equality under law. These are the literal builders who work with both their minds and their hands, making and repairing things in an economy that has prioritized the financial sector over the rest of its enterprises.

But these proud citizens have been ostracized and largely sidelined. They exert incredible leadership and influence at the micro level, of course. They are brave parents, choosing to confront corrupt educational systems that seek to poison the minds of their children. They challenge toxic and dishonest narratives that see the world though a concocted lens of oppressor versus oppressed. In their households, they sow the seeds to carry a society forward. But on the macro level, because of the new rules constructed by the Left, these white patriots have little influence. With the left-wing takeover of institutions, from big business to media to academia, it becomes exceedingly difficult for informed white citizens to move culture or policy since they lack any "forcefield protection."

So, with America in serious and systemic decline, nearly 60 percent of the national population has been rendered ineffective to truly forge the culture and laws in a way necessary to resurrect our floundering society. The largest demographic in society now incredibly has the least true power and the toughest time shaping any grand American revival. Straight white men have become especially useless in this obscene "brave new world" order, even though there are over one hundred million such citizens in America!

White men founded America. White people largely built this country, especially in the earliest era. But white citizens will not be able to save the republic now, despite strength in numbers.

So what about black Americans, can they act as saviors for our great land?

Unfortunately, the leadership class of black America has thoroughly poisoned the well of public discourse by constantly pumping anti-American and anti-white myths. As such, even patriotic, authentic, salt of the earth black citizens cannot seize enough influence to truly alter the course of America for the better.

I want to be crystal clear on this point: I do not suggest that regular, hardworking, God-fearing black citizens are somehow genetically or even culturally unable to do the hard work of forging a national renaissance. In fact, those hearty black citizens are the Americans most betrayed by the corrupted black leadership class.

For a window into the toxic messaging and dark hearts of that black leadership class, simply turn on MSNBC at just about any time of day or night. The anchors and guests engage in nonstop public relations campaigns for the Democratic Party, intermixed with a constant flow of mythmaking that demonizes whites. They act in direct contravention to the teachings of Martin Luther King Jr., who regularly challenged America to live up to the lofty goals of the American founding. He always and everywhere reaffirmed the clear worthiness of those ideals. Yet these modern influencers constantly deride America as intrinsically rotten and hopelessly compromised since our founding.

This distinction is clear. Martin Luther King Jr. goaded America with a correcting but also self-reinforcing message, saying, "America, you're better than this." But the so-called civil rights leaders of today promote a very different message, one that claims, "America, you are rotten to the core and you owe us. Pay up."

Though these media charlatans claim to be the heirs to Martin Luther King Jr., they campaign on a diametrically opposite philosophy that indicts and shames America as systemically malevolent and even irredeemable. From Hillary Clinton to Al Sharpton, these propagandists insult the inherent, aspirational goodness of America as a nation and as an ideal. At the same time, they rear their heads against the masses of Americans who happen to disagree with their bile.

Sadly, far too many cultural, academic, and business leaders of black America buy fully into this toxic line of thinking. One such influential figure is Nikole Hannah-Jones, leader of the ahistorical "The 1619 Project" conjured up by the *New York Times*. This ludicrous perversion of history rewrites the American past to pretend that our country was founded not in righteous rebellion against tyranny, but instead to spread slavery in the New World.

This *New York Times* effort demonstrates dishonest marketing from the most important newspaper in America. It is a shameless ploy to curry favor with radicals, especially among black leftists and self-loathing white radicals. Sadly, the campaign has largely succeeded, especially among black Americans looking for easy explanations and white radicals with dad issues.

Nikole Hannah-Jones appears regularly as a featured guest on corporate media platforms, explaining why America was never good, much less great. Despite her education at the University of Notre Dame, professorship at the University of North Carolina, and experience writing for the *New York Times*, this country has somehow, inexplicably, been terrible to her...and to those like her?

In point of fact, wouldn't a "systemically racist" country actually suppress the advancement of someone like Hannah-Jones, no matter her underlying skills or talents? Even though her own influence belies the crux of her arguments, "The 1619 Project" inflicted significant cultural and educational damage on America. It helped convince an entire generation of young Americans that our land was not founded by George Washington in constitutional order with the highest goals. According to this pervasive, insidious, and widely-dispersed myth, America was effectively founded as one giant slave enterprise.

Like Hannah-Jones, Mara Gay also found fame and influence at the *New York Times* by constantly coddling interviews on corporate media platforms. She espouses a similarly pollutive message about the foundational racism of America, citing her myopic Brooklyn worldview rather than reality.

She and Brian Williams once engaged, on-air, in a bout of mathematical nonsense that would embarrass a third-grade math student. Williams pointed out that Michael Bloomberg spent a gargantuan $500 million on his miserable failure of a presidential campaign. They then explained that such an amount could have instead granted $1 million to every single American, with plenty of cash leftover.[5] Of course, America does not have a population of 327 people to make this assertion true. No...America has a population of 327 *million* people, meaning that Bloomberg's pile of money would equal $1.53 per person. So...enough for a hot dog at Costco. Which is not exactly the same thing as one million dollars (Dr. Evil voice).

But the more revealing clip of Mara Gay, one that starkly conveyed her own deep-seeded antipathy for America, was another MSBC appearance on *Morning Joe*. She told host Mika Brzezinski that she was out on Long Island on a summer weekend in June 2021 and found it "just disturbing" to see "dozens of American flags."[6]

American flags! Some even on pickup trucks. Imagine?

Clearly, such people have neither the intellectual rigor nor the intentional motivation to return America to greatness. It is impossible to save any institution you actually hate, whether a school, a sports team, a company, or a country. Though the vast majority of black citizens in America love our country, they have been manipulated, misled, and overwhelmed by a black ruling class that shows no interest in building a society of comity.

In contrast, Asian Americans on the whole generally succeed in America, especially in academics and business, and they are growing as an important demographic with patriotic impulses. But the Asian communities of America are still too small to exert

---

5 Tim Hains, "MSNBC's Brian Williams, NYT's Mara Gay Agree Bloomberg Could Have Given Each American $1 Million With Money He Spent" (Real Clear Politics, March 6, 2020), https://www.realclearpolitics.com/video/2020/03/06/msnbcs_brian_williams_new_york_times_editorial_board_member_mara_gay_five_divided_by_three_equals_one_million.html

6 Steve Cortes (@CortesSteve), "So @MaraGay is 'disturbed' by American flags...and also apparently by mathematics" (X, June 8, 2021), https://x.com/CortesSteve/status/1402329343972581381.

critical mass. In addition, Asians have not yet assumed key positions of cultural power in this country, though they almost surely will in the near future.

So, if whites have been neutered (largely through self-inflicted wounds), the black ruling class hates America, and Asians lack numbers, then we are left with...Hispanics!

Let me make a key point here, early in this book. Readers may be saying to themselves, "Cortes is generalizing a lot about very large groups of people." This is a valid objection, and I grant that you are correct! Any serious discussion of large demographics must necessarily involve some level of generalization. Of course, the differences at the individual, family, or even community levels can be material in a giant nation of 330 million citizens. But I endeavor in all my work, including this book, to back large-scale theses with rigorous statistics, evidence-based rationales, and logical inferences. So, am I generalizing on many points? Absolutely! But are these generalizations nonetheless connected to objective, numerical realties? Also, absolutely.

Getting back to the reality of our country today and the potential for national rebirth, the United States could not be more fortunate to have such a widespread, vibrant Hispanic community, poised to star in this movie of American restoration.

Consider, for example, how America and Europe are differently situated in this regard. Europe unfortunately suffers from maladies that are similar to those that presently plague the United States. In fact, regarding issues of confidence and optimism for the future, ennui in Europe pervades. The Old World has even less hope than America does. Moreover, at least in Western Europe, any real sense of nationalism is mostly regarded as a racist, retrograde force. By contrast, in the United States, enlightened populist nationalism has essentially taken over one of the two dominant political parties.

But in terms of national renewal for countries like Spain, France, and Germany, they all lack what we have—a giant cohort of recent immigrants who love their new land and can lead a social renaissance. In fact, Europe faces the exact opposite situation. Almost all the immigration in the continent flows from the Muslim world, and assimilation has been practically nonexistent. Instead, the nations of Western Europe stand idly by as entire quasi-countries are constructed within their own borders. Huge swaths of migrants arrive at places like Italy and Belgium and hate their new host country. That situation seems illogical. Why immigrate to a place you reject? Well the truth is those migrants to Europe want the generous benefits and creature comforts of Europe, but without becoming European themselves. Nonetheless, they certainly enjoy those generous government welfare payments, allowing them to indulge in relative affluence in the pleasant capital cities created by great Europeans of the past.

But here in America, we have been blessed with a massive demographic of hardworking, patriotic, Christian immigrants from Latin America. From our earliest days as a colony to our inauguration as a true country, Latinos have been an incredible gift to this nation. It is hard to exaggerate the way people of Latin American heritage have affected the United States. From culture to the trades to food, Latinos have been a key pillar of American success, and their influence is vast—and growing.

Consider the good fortune of America in this regard. Of course, many of us believe that good fortune is God-ordained. But regardless of the source, the welcome reality of our country proves the truth of American exceptionalism.

A big part of this exceptionalism revolves around geography. We are a nation blessed with unmatched natural resources. Our country's interior has massive expanses of some of the most fertile lands in the world. Beneath the surface of our verdant soils lie vast deposits of fossil fuels and minerals. All these resources can be transported on a network of navigable rivers that are an international envy. In fact, the American landmass—more of a continent than a country, geographically speaking—offers a variety of climates and gorgeous topographies that have drawn migrants and tourists for centuries.

In addition, America is strategically a country that you would invent if you could play God. We are guarded by massive oceans on each flank. To the north lies a heavily forested region that abuts a friendly, culturally indistinguishable neighbor. Though the southern border region is naturally less hospitable, but since the days of the Mexican-American War, the United States and Mexico have lived in general comity and friendship for most of the last two centuries...at least until recent years with the current border crisis.

This friendly neighbor has exerted great influence upon the United States, both culturally and economically. In many ways, the two nations have melded into one quasi-country that dominates North America. For example, if you travel to American neighborhoods near the southern border and then cross over the Mexican side, the differences are generally immaterial. Further, even in regions far away from the border, Mexican industry, culture, food, and more hold great influence—all for the benefit of the United States.

But the most important "export" from Latin America by far has been people. Approximately sixty million Americans trace their ancestry to Latin America. Over the decades, tens of millions of legal immigrants, my own father amongst them, have come to the United States, assimilated while adding cultural depth, and enthusiastically rallied this great nation.

These legal Latin migrants bring vestiges of their homelands with them, of course. They also rightly show pride in most elements of their heritage. But these immigrants do not want to replicate the problems of Latin America here in the United States. People like my father, for example, know better than anyone that they came here for a reason—to escape the corruption, violence, and lack of opportunity that plagues most of our southern neighbors.

Quite unlike Europe, we are blessed with a recent immigrant demographic that not only appreciates its new American homeland, but also fully loves it. But here in America, we have the incredible benefit of tens of millions of Hispanics who are overwhelmingly Christian, hardworking, family-focused, and patriotic.

What a gift?!

Now, realize my appreciation for the giant Hispanic community in the United States does not, in any fashion, mean that porous borders are a good idea. In fact, the opposite reality must dominate our thinking and our patriotic populist agenda going forward. We must recognize that the Biden/Harris torrent of illegal migration across his open border is most offensive to legal immigrants who came here the right way. Immigrating to the United States is a lengthy and expensive process. The naturalized patriots who did it legally and properly out of respect for their new homeland are reviled at the prospect of mass illegal migration.

Legal migrants, such as my father, are not the only ones shocked by this injustice. Any rational American should be astounded by these current masses who trespass the border. We teach little toddlers not to hop the line because it is unfair. Why should we tolerate this present crisis of mass migration via a human tsunami of trespassers who enter into our homeland on their own terms? Just like any homeowner, we have every right and obligation to determine the rules about who enters our national home.

The globalists would have us believe that boundaries are ephemeral and vague. This is actually a rejection of the very basis of the nation-state. They have never accepted the Westphalian construct of sovereign nations that has allowed the United States and peer countries to flourish.

In addition, because of the chaotic nature of the border rush invited by Joe Biden and Kamala Harris, we have lost all ability to filter and judge the character, skills, and motives of those entering our homeland. This process should be rigorous, and it formerly was! By contrast, we now have millions of unknown migrants pouring into this land, many of whom are not properly vetted, and some of whom come with malicious intent.

One such cretin is Jose Antonio Ibarra, who crossed Joe Biden's open border from Venezuela before receiving taxpayer-funded transport to New York City. In that so-called sanctuary city, he received a criminal charge for endangering a child; this was his second offense, subsequent to his illegal entry into America without permission. Despite this charge, he was released into America's streets instead of facing deportation.

Then he moved to yet another so-called sanctuary city—Athens, Georgia. There he was also arrested, this time nabbed for shoplifting. But, once again, he was not deported and continued to roam the streets of our homeland despite his preventable crimes against Americans. He then massively increased his treachery when he crushed the skull of Laken Riley, a beautiful twenty-two-year-old nursing student who was jogging in broad daylight on the University of Georgia campus.

This crime shocked Americans who learned of the details, but too few Americans were informed. This story was largely hidden by the corrupt corporate media because it was so destructive to the ruling-class narrative about open borders. But Joe Biden was confronted about this tragedy during his 2024 State of the Union Address, and he responded by calling the victim "Lincoln Riley" instead of using her actual name, Laken Riley.

Biden also admitted that the arrested killer was "illegal." This plain acknowledgement of fact was simply too much for the woke Left, though, and Biden later apologized and retracted that accurate description! His White House and allied leftist groups now routinely refer to illegal migrants who break-and-enter in America as "guests," "newcomers," and "the undocumented." All those phrases are insulting, but the last might be the worst, since it suggests that some sort of paperwork is merely missing. Wrong. They are not "undocumented." They are unwelcome, unlawful, and unfairly here, and they harm the security and prosperity of American citizens, including Hispanic ones.

But, aside from that massive exception of illegals, the greater legal Hispanic community still represents a true gift to America—and the best hope looking forward to resurrecting American greatness.

Luckily for all Americans, Hispanics as a population display the correct traits and characteristics to indeed act as the new leadership vanguard to save the country. I make this statement as a proud Hispanic myself, but more importantly as a proud American. Throughout this book, I will alternately speak of Hispanics as a group from the third person, but also add in my own personal reflection as a Latino, myself. Luckily for Hispanics, we get the welcome burden of pulling off a magnificent feat, one that can pay dividends for generations long after we are gone from this earth. This book will explain the key reasons to believe that Hispanics will rise to this momentous task.

Though great challenges lie ahead, Hispanics can accomplish this mission. Unlike white Americans, we are not saddled with an unreasonable guilt about supposed privilege. In fact, the opposite is true. Hispanics generally enjoy the societal invincibility of minority status that has become the top pedestal of society in the twisted rules of post-Obama America. This "brown protection" grants far greater weight to the influence of Hispanics in culture, politics, media, and so forth. But unlike black Americans who suffer from the corruption of black elites who push nonsense and self-serving narratives, no similar Hispanic superseding class exists. At least not yet!

We cannot assume simple, Pollyanna-like expectations that such a perverse Hispanic class could not quickly develop. It could. Without the right leadership of God-fearing, America-loving Hispanic leaders, such a polluted Hispanic ruling class would materialize, and the Robin DiAngelos and Larry Finks of the world would be all too happy to co-opt such a politicized group. But the point I am making here is that such a poisoned influencer class has not yet asserted itself within the Hispanic community in America—and this opening provides incredible opportunity for Latinos in 2024 and beyond in this great country.

I strongly believe that the evidence and data, at both the anecdotal and macro levels, point to a broad and sustained renaissance of America led by Hispanics. From the leadership of the country to the headship of the home, Hispanics grow in influence, confidence, resources, and numbers. Consequently, as we examine the movement to restore America, we will find that bad hombres are leading the forefront of this national renaissance.

THE HISPANIC PARADOX

Do we have the guts and the vision to build the society we want? Very few Americans would argue that the country we love so dearly is currently doing well. In survey after survey, three-quarters of Americans or more concur that America is headed on the "wrong track."[7]

These already depressing numbers are even lower for young Americans. The future of America right now finds few reasons for optimism and hope. Consider the alarming findings of a recent NBC News poll of young Americans. For those aged eighteen to thirty-four, only 32 percent say patriotism is very important to them, compared to 76 percent of Baby Boomers.[8] Only 23 percent of the younger demographic report that having children is very important to them. No wonder the national birth rate plunges lower. We used to be exceptional on that metric, especially compared to other industrial nations, but not anymore.

---

7 "Satisfaction with the United States," *Gallup*, August 2, 2024, news.gallup.com/poll/1669/general-mood-country.aspx.

8 Noah Bressner and Mike Allen, "Jarring generation gap: America is divided on values, economics, politics" (Axios, May 21, 2024), https://www.axios.com/2024/05/21/us-generation-polls-economy-middle-east-politics.

That same NBC survey found that only one-third of young Americans believe that America is the best place to live—exactly half of the number of older Americans. That negative sentiment is not merely the result of youth ennui or a generational attitude problem, but rather reflects a society that is largely rigged in favor of an entrenched ruling class that is comprised almost completely of older, credentialed elites.

The ramifications of such a jaded society extend beyond sentiment, of course. Every salient measure of a healthy society deteriorates in America today, from overall longevity, to deaths caused by despair, to regular social interactions. I elucidate the scale and scope of the problems here not to wallow in self-pity or systemic sorrow, but rather to ignite a political, cultural, and societal fire that can illuminate the path up and out from this present quagmire.

After all, America is worth saving, in spite of the myriad afflictions that necessitate that very salvific act! America at her best is the beacon of hope for this fallen world. With all our present maladies, America still represents the enduring dream for mankind on this earth.

In addition, from a purely practical standpoint, there is no viable alternative to America. We want to save this country and must do so first and foremost because we love her with all our hearts. But we must also save America because there is no safety valve, no "other America," to which we can escape. As Cuban refugee and Florida businessman Maximo Alvarez so movingly remarked to the Republican National Convention in 2020, "I choose America...because there is no other place to go."[9]

---

9 Maximo Alvarez, "Speech at the Republican National Convention: 2020 RNC Night 1" (PBS NewsHour, August 24, 2020), https://www.youtube.com/watch?v=jJnShBMG3uY&t=375s.

Moreover, the memory of America's former greatness can serve as a propellant and accelerant to a national renewal. A great athlete who falls into bad habits but then regenerates himself will have an easier time reclaiming physical prowess than someone who never knew greatness at all.

But such a national renewal requires two important ingredients. First, we must summon the will to restore America. Second, there must be a group of people willing to own leadership over that restoration. That group does not have to comprise the majority of society; it simply must be a large enough group to affect change and move the national needle back toward greatness.

In this time and place—America in the 2020s—who is that group?

It's Hispanics. In fact, it can only be Hispanics.

Will Hispanics truly be the patriots to save America? It seems like a paradox to believe that a bunch of (mostly) newly migrated people who came from the largely troubled countries south of the United States will resurrect and restore the great American experiment that was started and fashioned by Northern European Protestants.

Is this seeming contradiction a reality, especially into a fulcrum election decision process in 2024?

Well, I believe—for reasons of evidence and data—that Hispanics will save America. I also believe *only* Hispanics can save America!

But before diving deeper into how Latinos will become the leadership bulwark of an American renaissance, it is instructive to look at another Hispanic paradox, one involving relative physical and mental vitality.

For decades, public health officials have noted how Latinos tend to have better health outcomes than other Americans, despite some serious structural differences that would normally point to poorer health. For example, Hispanics are poorer than white Americans overall, and yet the incidence of preventable death prior to old age is identical to white Americans.[10]

That same breakdown of data shows, moreover, that Latinos have a far lower rate of early, preventable deaths as compared to black Americans. Because of lower economic prosperity and a more entrepreneurial culture, Hispanics overall have less access to traditional employer-based healthcare, and that deficiency is further exacerbated by Hispanics who are not here legally. Nonetheless, the macro health outcomes are good, right in line with or even preferable to those of white Americans.

This Hispanic paradox was first noted by academics in 1986 with a groundbreaking study from two professors at the University of Texas. As noted by the American Heart Association, Professors "Kyriakos Markides and Jeannine Coreil published their analysis of two decades' worth of studies." The teachers determined that "Hispanic people in the Southwest fared better in key health indicators, including death due to cardiovascular diseases and some types of cancer."[11]

Reacting to this surprising data, Luisa Borrell, professor in the graduate program in epidemiology and biostatistics at the

---

[10] Maya Goldman, "Racial health disparities exist in every state, new report says" (Axios, April 18, 2024), https://www.axios.com/2024/04/18/racial-health-disparities-every-state?utm_source=newsletter&utm_medium=email&utm_campaign=newsletter_axioslatino&stream=science.

[11] Lourdes Medrano, "The 'Hispanic paradox': Does a decades-old finding still hold up?" (American Heart Association, May 10, 2023), https://www.heart.org/en/news/2023/05/11/the-hispanic-paradox-does-a-decades-old-finding-still-hold-up.

City University of New York, observed that "despite the fact that Hispanics as a group have lower education, lower income and less access to health care, their health outcomes are much better or similar to the white population."[12]

In fact, even as overall longevity started to decline in the United States before the coronavirus panic, longevity rates for Hispanics remained steady, at eighty-two years old in 2019 as compared to seventy-nine for whites.[13]

So what explains this Latino health paradox, this comparative vitality? For starters, it must be acknowledged that there is no easy, singular explanation...or else the phenomenon would not be regarded as a "paradox!"

That point conceded, we can make some reasonable and educated guesses about this apparently illogical health performance among Latinos. Part of the explanation almost certainly involves the commitment to work and exertion of the Hispanic community. As a demographic of doers, Latinos generally embrace more rigorous lives than other demographics, often including strenuous physical work that builds strong bodies as well as spirits.

In addition, Hispanics enjoy this paradox of performance in mental and physical health because of stronger social bonds compared to other Americans. Despite material hurdles due to lower socioeconomic status, Hispanics embrace family and communal life at levels above those of other demographics. The average Hispanic household, for example, accommodates an extra person on average. This reality alone is enough to foster more interactions, especially on a national scale, when factoring in tens of millions of Hispanic citizens.

---

[12] Ibid.

[13] Ibid.

Hispanics rely on interpersonal connectivity and relationships in an outsized way compared to credentialed white America. NYU Stern researcher Zach Rausch remarked about this sad trend in broader American society, saying, "We have long been moving into a world of increased convenience and pleasure, at the cost of strong and local tight-knit communities—which has led to profound isolation and loneliness.... We must find ways to provide children with vibrant 'community-based childhoods' if we want to replace the placeless and harmful 'phone-based childhood.'"[14]

Hispanics have largely already solved this problem. But even more importantly, their focus on family relations, extended relatives, and stronger community bonds make Hispanics an overall healthier and happier population—one poised to lead an American renaissance. Within this new reality lies a paradox that almost belies history.

Why?

Because for nearly a century, the middle history of America was dominated by the philosophy of Manifest Destiny. This overarching driving force of American life, from the early 1800s until the early 1900s, demanded that the United States occupy and subdue all of the North American continent, from the Atlantic to Pacific Coast. This narrative and ethos helped guide America's conquest and purchase of the lands formerly colonized by Spain or held by Mexico.

---

[14] Zach Rausch (@ZachMRausch), "We have long been moving into a world of increased convenience and pleasure, at the cost of strong and local tight-knit communities" (X, June 10, 2024), https://x.com/zachmrausch/status/1800270052974825601?s=43&t=sdb0eiXZMxMwKucb7qtlOA.

Now, more than a century and a half after the conclusion of the Mexican-American War, it is indeed the offspring of Mexico who will form the driving tip of the spear to save America itself.

How is such a transformation possible?

First, the failures of Latin America dictate that the United States exists as its opposite, acting as a safety valve for the best and brightest of Latin America who strive for more than a life of mediocrity and societal corruption. In this regard, those who largely conquered Latin America now culturally conquer North America—not through compulsion, but rather through culture and life force.

Because the failed countries of Latin America never provided hopeful opportunities such as those promised to the European conquerors and settlers of Spanish America, it is almost inevitable that the descendants of these settlers would eventually look north for the possibilities denied to them in the Southern hemisphere.

This new reality, too, forms part of the paradox of Hispanics saving America. Imagine our ancestors even considering this notion—the descendants of the vanquished Latin America would become the saviors of the American order, the white Anglo-Saxon experiment of the United States.

But this place is exactly where we are today, in large part because the WASPs (white Anglo-Saxon Protestants) who formed America's ruling class for centuries have not only foresworn a duty to make America great, but they now despise the very idea of American greatness.

In other words, the same groups that formed and idealized American exceptionalism now revile and belittle it. Conversely, the group most harmed by the implementation of that exceptionalism, historically speaking, now becomes the lead vanguard of an

American renewal that refocuses our nation around exceptional and unapologetic truth.

In this regard, America beholds and embraces a new frontier. From its founding days until roughly a century ago, a large part of the American experience and character was formed by a drive for expansion, stretching ever westward toward the Pacific Ocean. The settlement of the continent animated a big part of the American ideal for many decades. Even citizens who never left the safer denizens of the East Coast benefitted from a country that pushed relentlessly West. The lessons and character of the nation were formed by the frontier, regardless of any individual's own frontier status.

Once that physical Western frontier closed, approximately just before World War I, America's national attention focused on new, global struggles. These issues of massive magnitude replaced, at least symbolically, the physical challenge of the Western frontier. Almost immediately after settling the western United States and establishing itself as a continental, Atlantic to Pacific superpower, America faced unprecedented international challenges. Our country fought and won two world wars and then engaged in the Cold War against global Marxism.

Throughout much of the twentieth century, these great struggles dominated America's culture and spurred the further advancement of America's greatness. The physical frontier of the American West was replaced with a metaphorical frontier, as America acted as the protector of Western Civilization against fierce global enemies.

However, with the end of the Cold War, America maintained a longstanding dominion over the trans-oceanic landmass, and it found itself without a great external struggle.

As such, America started to decay both culturally and physically. On that latter point, when did America last build something on a truly grand scale, something that will last and be admired for generations? Is there any Hoover Dam or Golden Gate Bridge project? Instead, America wastes billions of dollars on a ridiculous, unused "train to nowhere" in California. But this kind of decay is a choice, even if it is the default option for most societies.

Chris Buskirk makes this point persuasively in his excellent book *America and the Art of the Possible: Restoring National Vitality in an Age of Decay*. Buskirk, who founded the nationalist platform American Greatness, argues that societies tend toward decay as a default option. In this fallen world, if strong volition is not exerted, countries and societies devolve rather than improve.

In Buskirk's analysis, both the prior challenges of the American frontier and the nation's global battles were profound enough to rally the citizens of the United States, leading them to create an ever-better society that defied the natural inclination toward decay. But now, in many ways, that battle turns inward. With a continent tamed and no immediate military threats to American hegemony (though China clearly stalks), what will become of this great country?

So far, we know too well the plans of the Marxist Democrats. That phrase may seem a bit extreme to many readers. Are the Democrats really Marxists? Unfortunately, yes. The Democrats of the 2020s are no longer the loyal opposition. These are not your parents' or grandparents' Democrats. Long gone are people like Harry Truman, John F. Kennedy, Mayor Richard J. Daley, and Henry "Scoop" Jackson. Today's Democratic Party proudly advocates for chopping the genitals off children and an open border that allows and invites an unchecked invasion from the rest of the world onto American soil.

These Marxists want to remake American society into a place that is unrecognizable to our ancestors.

Skeptics may presume that the views of those ancestors are simply antiquated and that our society has somehow improved, progressing past those narrow views held by previous generations. But my favorite author, G.K. Chesterton, makes a compelling case that tradition matters and ought to bind us as the "democracy of the dead." In other words, our predecessors' decisions matter, and the dead effectively get a vote on what happens in our society long after their passing from this earth.

Well, if the deceased do indeed get to vote, then they would be very unhappy indeed with the current state of American society. Just as importantly, the American citizens of today are also very unhappy with our society. We are, without question, a despairing group of people, as proven by every relevant survey as well as the metrics of social pathologies that afflict our land.

Despite this depressed mood and general dissatisfaction, the muscle memory of American greatness remains strong and well-entrenched. As a naturally optimistic people, we refuse to submit to this decay, and an important vanguard forms that will not crumble under the seemingly inevitable moral, cultural, and economic decline prescribed by the American ruling class.

This vanguard is largely composed of Hispanics and especially Latino men. These bad hombres are the leaders, for example, against the expanding financial sector currently dominating the American economy. Through decades of policy errors, this country now places an obscene premium on financial engineering rather than physical engineering.

But Hispanics, especially Hispanic men, form the counter-revolution to this unfortunate trend. Latino men—bad hombres—are the ones who know how to physically build great edifices and make things. If America makes the necessary change to prioritize domestic production in the coming years, then Hispanics will take lead roles in the re-establishment of America as a great industrial power. Globalization has utterly failed America in every way. Those failures were exposed during the irrational COVID-19 panic, when many Americans realized just how much we rely on overseas supply lines to source many of our most critical products, from semiconductors to medicines.

Restoring domestic production in the United States is both an economic and a national security imperative. This process will be possible and successful largely because of Hispanics generally and Hispanic men particularly.

Regarding politics and the upcoming 2024 elections, Hispanics will play the decisive role in returning the country to a populist nationalist trajectory. In the key swing states, particularly those in the Sun Belt, Hispanics occupy the places of political kingmakers. In Arizona, Nevada, and Georgia in particular, Hispanics will determine the presidential winner.[15]

Not many people think of Georgia as all that Hispanic, by the way, but it is! Georgia has over one million Hispanics.[16] The Latin population there has exploded in the last two decades. The Peach State has long been a production center and a home of good red

---

[15] Andrea Flores, "Latinx Files: What Does the Electorate Look Like in Key Swing States?" De Los, August 16, 2024, latimes.com/delos/newsletter/2024-08-16/Latinx-files-latino-vote-swing-states-presidential-election-latinx-files.

[16] UCLA Latino Policy and Politics Institute, "15 Facts About Latino Well-Being in Georgia" (UCLA Latino Policy and Politics Institute, August 24, 2022), https://latino.ucla.edu/research/15-facts-latinos-georgia/.

state governance, which has led to ample employment growth. My people go where the jobs are!

Into the election, bad hombres and proud Latinas in Atlanta, Phoenix, and Las Vegas will provide the margin of victory for President Trump to retake the White House and serve a second term that will prove beneficial for all America broadly and for Latinos specifically.[17]

A Trump presidency has further economic promise for Hispanics. Hedge fund mogul Scott Bessent spoke on this in a recent address to the Manhattan Institute regarding the failures of Bidenomics, where he also encouraged a return to the policies that produced the Trump Boom before the virus panic of 2020. Bessent may very well become Trump's Treasury Secretary in a second Trump term. Further, Bessent was a former top trader for George Soros, of all people.

Though Bessent and Soros share the skill of managing money well, they clearly do not share a political philosophy! Bessent pointed out, for example, that Hispanic pay leaped to the front of wage gains during the Trump presidency, rising 4.5 percent in real terms (adjusted for inflation).[18] Now, during the Biden presidency, real wages have declined overall because of the massive, systemic Biden inflation that robs hardworking Americans of buying power. For Hispanics, this Bidenomics failure hits especially hard, with real wages down 0.7 percent so far.

Clearly we cannot accept such mediocrity. We are Americans, and we cannot become comfortable with smaller families, smaller

---

17 "Donald Trump Poised to Win More Latino Votes than Any Republican in Recent History," *Newsweek*, July 9, 2024, newsweek.com/Donald-trump-latino-votes-presidential-election-1921384

18 Scott K.H. Bessent, "The Fallacy of Bidenomics: A Return to Central Planning" (Manhattan Institute, June 6, 2024), https://manhattan.institute/article/the-fallacy-of-bidenomics-a-return-to-central-planning.

paychecks, and smaller goals. If we are to spur a national renewal, Hispanics must occupy the frontline leadership of that renaissance. Only Hispanics have the characteristics and the drive to lead a great American restoration.

Time magazine founder and media magnate Henry Luce called the 1900s the "American Century." He was right—American values dominated those times. But what about now and the future? Well, with faith in God Almighty and an unchallenged belief in the potential of America, the second American Century of the 2000s will unfold with proud Hispanics leading the way.

MY STORY

March 16, 2017. I stepped foot into the Oval Office for the first time in my life.

Seeing it in person provides quite a rush, especially for anyone involved in politics. After watching countless live television feeds from that hallowed office and endless political dramas and comedies, I knew the layout of the world's most famous office well, and entering nonetheless instilled a sense of awe, at least for the first visit.

I arrived to talk strategy with the newly inaugurated forty-fifth president of the United States, a man I had worked tirelessly to help elect throughout 2016. Incidentally, when I say I "worked" for Trump in 2016, I more precisely mean "volunteered." I gave up a paid cable TV gig to volunteer as a spokesman for the upstart campaign. I left the comfortable routine of working as a contributor on Fox News, which is reasonably smooth sailing for a right-wing commentator. I was soon dispatched by Team Trump to the most difficult and contentious interviews, especially on CNN and MSNBC. I appeared on the latter network almost daily from summer 2016 until election day, including the morning after the election. In that interview, believe it or not, they permitted me to gloat on-air about then-President-elect Trump's "massive upset victory."

Wow, have times changed. In 2020, I joined President Trump's professional campaign staff for reelection. Over the many months I served as Senior Advisor for Strategy, I think I only did a handful of MSNBC hits. That paucity of appearances shows how the legacy media approach to Trump changed once he actually defeated Hillary Clinton. Until that time, Trump was a novelty and ratings were clickbait gold for these media platforms, including the unfriendly ones (which was all the legacy organizations).

But once Trump shocked all the newsrooms in New York and the lobbying offices on K Street in Washington, the tone and substance changed…and fast! Once the reality of a populist nationalist in office really took hold, we were mostly shut out of any serious interviews, and we were certainly excluded from any evenhanded coverage.

But back in 2016, when the mainstream media was still willing, even eager, to play ball with Team Trump, I was in high demand as a surrogate. Truth be told, I loved the challenge of facing off against antagonistic press partisans live on-air. It was challenging and mostly fun. It really sharpened my TV skills and forced me to become a better communicator.

All that said, by the end of the campaign season I was physically and mentally exhausted. I have never worked so hard, even for something I was paid to do, as I did as a volunteer for Trump in 2016. But I believed from the top of my head down to the tips of my toes that we were quickly losing our country. I further believed then, as I do now, that only a return to enlightened populist nationalism, in the spirit of Teddy Roosevelt and Abraham

Lincoln, could claw back our republic from the oligarchs who were increasingly controlling and punishing middle America.

As sort of media healing process to that exhaustion, I went back to Fox News as a contributor for all of 2017. The network needed Trump voices, and I was happy to oblige. My wife was just thankful I was getting paid again! With my wife at home with four young children, revenue in the door is not merely a luxury for Team Cortes, but a necessity.

So I went back to my Wall Street career full-time and did politics and media on the side. I was a busy man, but it was nothing compared to the boiler-room-feel of 2016. This formed the backdrop for my visit to the White House for the first time since being there on a school trip as a kid.

As I walked into the Oval Office, I immediately thought of my late father. For a brief moment, I entered almost a trance-like state where I imagined him there with me. I know that statement might sound strange, but it was very real to me immediately when I stepped into the Oval Office. Hopefully I did not appear confused to the new president!

With my dad on my mind, I started to wonder. Was Alfonso Cortes, as an immigrant to this land, beaming with pride that his son earned his way into the company of the president of his adopted homeland? Does he look down from heaven and know I am here? Did I fulfill his personal American dream by becoming a confidant of the president of the United States?

By dream, by the way, I mean the actual, affirmative American dream of my father and millions of legal immigrants like him—the patriotic vision of assimilation and contribution to the American republic. This very real dream contrasts sharply with Barack

Obama's illusory *Dreams from My Father*, which helped pave the way for his run for political office, culminating in his presidency.

Obama's father's dreams involved castigating America and, more broadly, all of the West. Barack Obama, Sr. became one of countless pseudo-intellectuals trained in American universities to pretend that Western Civilization equates to some grand tyranny. Moreover, he explained away any problems of the underdeveloped world, including his own Kenya, as the supposed lingering consequences of colonization.

As I discussed in the opening chapter of this book, far too many black leaders and influencers have abused their positions of power and betrayed the masses of the proud, hardworking black citizens they claim to represent. Although not an American, Obama's father gladly joined in with this cohort of black intellectuals who gained accelerated access to the highest levels of American society as part of explicit, de facto affirmative action initiatives. But so many of them used that access simply for self-aggrandizement. Others used those opportunities to promote Marxist, secular humanist ideas, which caused far more harm to black communities than the previous eras of systemic oppression ever did.

In the specific case of Obama's father, if he had inkling of a conscience, imagine how different his own life would have been, and, by extension, the formation of Barack Obama. If Barack Obama, Sr. could have mustered even a modicum of self-introspection, perhaps he would have realized that America afforded incredible opportunities for him. He attended graduate school at Harvard, the most prestigious university in the United States. Instead of using that incredible springboard to improve the lives of American blacks or his own Kenyan countrymen, he instead operated as a typical selfish leftist.

For example, he abandoned his son—the future president—at the age of two, only seeing him one other time for the rest of young Barack's life.

My own father embraced the promise and goodness of America in direct opposition to the false victim narrative of Barack Obama, Sr. In a strange sense, though, Obama led directly to my own West Wing experience. After all, his polished but divisive two terms crushed the American middle class. This supposed progressive caused a massive exacerbation of economic inequality, rewarding his corporatist sponsors and pushing a constant agenda of globalism alongside his committed, multilateralist vice president Joe Biden.

The failures of the Obama-Biden tenure—especially those relating to trade, the economic ravaging of American industry, and the demise of the American middle class—led directly to the Tea Party movement. That cause, in turn, metastasized into the populist nationalism of the America First movement, which found its indispensable national instrument in the candidacy of Donald J. Trump.

Working-class people of all races and ethnicities rallied to this agenda of national sovereignty, cultural conservatism, and the diffusion of economic power. Perhaps the most surprising coverts, at least to the permanent Washington political class, were Hispanic Americans. Bad hombres.

A trip to the near past provides context to explain my role in this process, to better understand where Hispanics are now politically, and to know where the trend points going forward.

As mentioned previously, the phrase "bad hombres" gained national attention during the hotly contested presidential election between Donald Trump and Hillary Clinton. Trump used the phrase during the third and final presidential debate in Las Vegas. I had attended the prior two debates, starting at Hofstra University on Long Island and then attending the infamous "Billy Bush Access Hollywood" debate in St. Louis at Washington University. For the third and final debate, I was watching on TV in a studio in my hometown of Chicago, preparing for several live remote national interviews occurring after the debate. As I watched that night, on October 19th, 2016, Trump again used the phrase: "We have some bad hombres here, and we're gonna get 'em out."[19]

It really grabbed me that time. First, because it perfectly encapsulated how Trump spoke. He was a brash New Yorker who spoke the truth with the bark on. He was direct, sometimes offensive, but always authentic. Given how badly the polite and polished operatives of the ruling class had been abusing regular Americans for decades, the gruff and real style of Trump was very welcome.

Additionally, he was unafraid to touch third rail issues. I, too, share that publicly intrepid approach, as evidenced by the theses presented in this very book! Look, there was a time in America, perhaps the 1980s and before, when the state of our country and health of our society were so impressive that only polite discourse was required.

After all, the conservatives and liberals of that bygone era coalesced and agreed on almost all foundational principles. The

[19] Lizzy Gurdus, "Trump: 'We have some bad hombres and we're going to get them out'" (CNBC, October 19, 2016), https://www.cnbc.com/2016/10/19/trump-we-have-some-bad-hombres-and-were-going-to-get-them-out.html.

only real showdowns were over the details or over the tactics deployed to reach commonly agreed-upon goals. We were a society and nation that largely agreed on first things—a consensus coming from a nation that was quite religious and dominated by Christian principles. Even citizens who were not Christian believers still largely subscribed to the mores and principles of Western Civilization as formed by centuries of Christian belief.

But from roughly the 1990s onward, huge chasms opened up and split American society apart. Now the differences between the Right and the Left are Grand Canyon-sized gaps. As an example, consider how radically the Democrat Party supports open borders. Compare recent statements from Biden and his allies to the pronouncements of politicians like Bill Clinton and even Barack Obama regarding border sovereignty.

As such, understanding the weight of current politics in America became a prerequisite for any politician on the Right. Trump understood this reality and seemed to actually relish the fight. After all, his battle was not only against Hillary and the toxic Democrat leadership but also against many Republicans. Our movement, at its core, opposed the American establishment that had morphed into a selfish, globalist cabal of elites who constantly attacked the prerogative of the formerly great American middle class.

In this kind of civilizational battle, there is little use for the politics of niceness, and tough talk must be combined with aggressive action. In addition, Trump grasped the importance of entertainment in politics for most voters. In this new digital media landscape, he was perfectly positioned to capture the constant opportunities of earned coverage, in part by making people laugh.

In this regard, "bad hombres" was a fun phrase that simply made people smile. While making a very important point about a deadly serious topic of open borders, Trump and our movement found a way to insert some levity, contributing to the influx of media attention.

So, that night of October 2016, then-private citizen Donald Trump uttered those words during the third and final presidential debate against Hillary Clinton before a Super Bowl-sized national television audience. By that time, even the haters of Trump could not get enough of his content. In fact, the haters might have been the *most* motivated to watch. Regardless, there he was, firing verbal rockets like "bad hombres" a mere three weeks before he would shock the political world with the most astounding upset win in American electoral history.

Prior to that point, throughout 2016, Trump had talked tough regarding the border, building a wall, and deporting dangerous bad hombres out of the United States. The American ruling class recoiled at these blunt terms and brash prescriptions. The elites, therefore, worked extra hard to brandish the America First movement as somehow racist or jingoistic. But much to the chagrin of the credentialed crony elites (almost none of whom are Latino), Hispanics form a key pillar of the burgeoning movement of patriotic populism across America.

In fact, as much as any other group, Hispanics—and especially Hispanic men—rally to the muscular political combination of economic populist nationalism and cultural conservatism. This book analyzes the antecedents of this massive, macroscopic, right-wing shift for Hispanics, and it provides a roadmap agenda for a future where the rising Hispanic constituency can build this movement into a dominant force in US politics for decades to come.

This move to the political Right involves much more than just Donald Trump, of course. As crucial as he was in proving the national appeal of patriotic populism, the movement preceded him and will surely thrive well beyond his political viability.

But Trump, though the permanent political class castigated him as somehow anti-Hispanic, clearly was a critical accelerant for this rightward shift. Hispanics, paradoxically, were gravitating toward him. Those well-scripted, crony class political veterans could not fathom the magnetism of Trump's authenticity, particularly for masses of working-class voters, many of whom happen to be Hispanic.

As explained above, when Trump called many of the illegal migrants that have poured into our homeland "bad hombres," he displayed exactly the kind of plain, tough talk that regular people appreciate.

Hispanics know, better than most, that some truly bad hombres have crossed illegally into America. Many of these individuals, like the monsters of transnational gangs like MS-13, wreak untold havoc on Hispanic communities in this country. Not surprisingly, Hispanic citizens of our country are the primary victims of dangerous illegal migrants who are allowed to hide in plain sight in so-called sanctuary cities. Dangerous illegals make life miserable for Hispanics in the United States. More broadly, even outside of the illegal immigration issue, Hispanics as a community have long believed in law and order in a particularly intense way. Hispanics proudly embrace law enforcement; they hold a steadily growing percentage of law enforcement jobs across America from federal immigration enforcement to local police forces.

Whether discussing decades of porous borders or transnational gangs, a large part of the success of this populist movement lies in communicating with directness and authenticity. Trump, as a seasoned TV star, excelled at this key task. He rejected the typical political formula of reciting tortured and lawyerly phrases from teleprompters. In response, Hispanics embraced his macho, direct, and sometimes gruff commentary.

The communications realm of TV broadcasting provided the avenue for my own entry into the movement. I worked for twenty-five years as an institutional broker and trader. I transacted in bond markets and stock market sector ETF's (exchange traded funds) for some of the largest hedge funds in existence, mostly domiciled in Europe.

My Wall Street career led to a TV gig with CNBC. First I was a frequent guest brought on to discuss capital markets. Then I was hired by the channel to serve as a daily on-air contributor, primarily as a cast member for the *Fast Money* shows at noon and 5 p.m. Eastern Time.

Though I never had TV aspirations and basically fell into my second career, my TV appearances significantly enhanced my existing Wall Street business and reputation. TV also provided a fun and challenging new pursuit. Debating stock tickers and markets on live TV everyday keeps the mind focused. The daily back-and-forth also sharpened my debating and broadcasting skills.

Learning the craft of doing TV well was difficult and, for me, harkened back to my days as a college football player. Just as on the gridiron, I watched tape, I practiced a lot, and I watched other players who were better than me. With a lot of "reps" and the constant excitement of capital markets, I grew into the role.

But all the while, the effects of government policy increased dramatically in the overall economy and in financial markets specifically. Understanding markets intrinsically meant discerning the next steps of an ever-reaching and controlling leviathan from Washington, DC. When I first started broadcasting, I kept my right-wing political leanings almost totally off the air. But over time the effects of the Great Recession and the disastrous policies of the Obama-Biden administration made such policy neutrality impossible for any honest market analyst or trader.

Unfortunately, CNBC increasingly surrendered journalistic and editorial control over to its parent company in Connecticut—General Electric. That massive conglomerate became so wedded to the Obama-Biden administration that it was practically a federal department. From bailouts to massive federal contracts to a full submission to the Obama-Biden leftist social agenda, General Electric went native with the leftist statists before most large companies.

As such, my views became discouraged and even muzzled. But by then, in 2015, I had established a reputation as a solid broadcaster and sharp market analyst. As such, I was recruited by many former CNBC colleagues who moved on to News Corp to help that media empire grow the fledgling Fox Business, the younger sister channel to Fox News.

By 2016 I started appearing regularly on Fox, mostly on shows with fellow alums of CNBC who had moved over, including Maria Bartiromo and Trish Regan. Unlike the NBC Universal media conglomerate, Fox welcomed my insights—not just on financial markets, but also on politics. Still, my primary focus on television was financial markets, and I talked a lot more about stock tickers than I did politicians.

As the 2016 race heated up, that focus would change dramatically. Little did I know that my TV skills would soon be devoted exclusively to politics and to promoting this burgeoning movement, particularly to Hispanic bad hombre audiences. In fact, a group of Hispanic men I did not even know played a primary role in pushing me toward this new career and mission.

When Trump first came down the escalator at Trump Tower to announce his candidacy for the presidency in 2015, I was admittedly skeptical and regarded it as a smart but insincere publicity gambit. But then a group of Hispanic strangers opened up my mind to seriously consider Trump. Late one night after appearing on Fox News at its headquarters in midtown Manhattan, I ate at a diner. As the hour was late, it was closing down, and I was the last customer.

The cooks and staff from the kitchen were watching a newscast of Trump's latest speech. They were all clearly Hispanic and conversing with one another in Spanish. They loved Trump. When I asked them why, they said "because he is successful and because he tells the truth."

These blue-collar Latinos made quite an impression on me. Number one, they admired his success. Number two, they embraced his straight talk. From that moment on, I started listening much more carefully to Trump and devouring populist literature and articles. Voices like Pat Buchanan and Steve Bannon resonated with me. The corrupt ruling class of America, which I previously regarded as basically sound, was crushing working-class citizens with reckless globalism, uncontrolled borders, and needless warfare all over the world.

My political shift from a Wall Street-style Republican to a fiery populist began in that New York diner with a needed nudge from some salt of the earth Latinos. In addition to my economic commentary on TV, I started regularly praising Donald Trump on-air and defending key new policy pillars like building a wall and ending overseas military adventurism.

My appearances were noticed over at Trump Tower, and I was soon invited into the campaign as a media surrogate—a spokesman doing TV and radio hits on behalf of the candidate.

In fact, I soon became the campaign's go-to broadcaster for the toughest interviews with the most adversarial and corrupt corporate media outlets. I tangled with biased left-wing pundits and hosts every single day of 2016 as the campaign heated up. With a smile, I battled the leftist luminaries of the corporate media—people like Don Lemon, Ana Navarro, and Chris Hayes.

I learned a lot about these "journalists" from my hundreds of interviews and behind-the-scenes moments in green rooms as I waited for appearances. Nearly all of these broadcasters acted dutifully as public relations agents for the Democrats and the ruling-class corporate elites. It also became massively apparent that these media mavens not only reviled Trump as an individual, but also the patriotic populist movement as a whole.

While their duplicity and lack of curiosity was appalling, it also provided opportunity. These smug New York and DC operators remained almost totally oblivious to the clear, material populist backlash that was building in America and had been for years. Our campaign analytics and my own street sense pointed to a strategy of opposing the press every bit as much as we opposed Hillary Clinton. The decades-long slow slide in public trust for legacy media began to careen lower in 2016. As such, spokesmen like me found ample opportunity to win over persuadable voters by highlighting the hypocrisy and aloofness of media charlatans, often right to their faces on their own shows on live television!

In this important task, I played a critical role as a Latino. I constantly defanged and deconstructed the abject media lie that border security is racist or that our America First movement represented some sort of stealth racism. Over time, I could almost hear the groans from NBC and CNN hosts when I prefaced my on-air responses with: "Well, as a Hispanic citizen…"

This massive disconnect between media stars and regular people was clearly not healthy for our society. Later in this book I will delve much deeper into the media landscape and the reasons for my cautious optimism regarding a transformed media going forward, especially with one geared toward Hispanics. But this chasm between New York newsrooms and middle America's reality in 2016 provided opportunity. The corporate media loved the ratings and controversy of Trump and this new political movement. At the same time, none of the decision-makers at places like ABC News or NPR actually thought the movement could win, so they willingly gave ample airtime for the always-entertaining Donald Trump as well as spokesmen for the movement like me.

Unwittingly, these legacy media leaders provided a needed opening for the movement to start reaching the masses, many of whom were either formerly Democrats or just apolitical. A huge section of those converts came from Hispanic America. This book details the massive rightward movements for Hispanics and how their momentum into the present day suggests further gains to come. Looking back, it is amazing to me that the spoiled and content globalists chose to stay comfortably ensconced in their establishment bubbles of New York newsrooms and Georgetown salons in DC. They were blissfully unperturbed by the growing disenchantment of working-class citizens, many of whom are Hispanics.

Despite incessant media narratives castigating Trump as some sort of Hispanic-hating modern Bull Connor, he held his own in 2016 among Hispanics, winning a respectable 28 percent of the Latino vote, essentially right in line with the previous two Republican nominees, Mitt Romney in 2012 and John McCain in 2008.[20] In contrast, Hilary Clinton lost 5 percent of Hispanic support compared to her predecessor nominee, President Obama.[21]

That 2016 Hispanic vote performance shocked the leftists who assumed that they simply own minority votes. But the trouble was just beginning for these smug operatives. Over the ensuing years, this solid base of Hispanic support grew measurably and now portends a groundswell of Hispanics at the forefront of the patriotic populist movement. Specifically, Trump earned a massive jump in overall Hispanic support in 2020 with 38 percent of the Latino vote, according to Pew Research Center's "validated voter" survey.[22]

There are many varied sources of information out there regarding statistics about the Hispanic vote. Most of those cited by the corporate media emanate from exit polls. Such polls do have some value. They are literally conducted as voters leave polling places. But they are not nearly as accurate as the Pew Research Center survey, which is really the gold standard of post-election analysis.

---

20 Jens Manuel Krogstad and Mark Hugo Lopez, "Hillary Clinton won Latino vote but fell below 2012 support for Obama" (Pew Research Center, November 29, 2016), https://www.pewresearch.org/short-reads/2016/11/29/hillary-clinton-wins-latino-vote-but-falls-below-2012-support-for-obama/.

21 Ibid.

22 Steven Shepard, "New poll shows how Trump surged with women and Hispanics—and lost anyway" (Politico, June 30, 2021), https://www.politico.com/news/2021/06/30/new-trump-poll-women-hispanic-voters-497199.

Of course, the best way to obtain totally reliable information on voting patterns is to examine actual vote totals. The problem here is that in many parts of the country, Hispanics do not live in highly concentrated areas, and so it becomes difficult, for example, to single out the Hispanic vote from the regular white vote. Whether or not a person votes is public information, but the decision they make at the ballot box is secret, of course.

But in some areas of the country where Hispanics are highly concentrated, we can derive very useful and accurate information about Latino voting trends over time.

In some of these key areas, the vote gains from 2016–2020 were most impressive. For example, in the most Hispanic county in America, Starr County on the Texas-Mexico border, Trump's four-year ascent seems almost too lofty to believe. In 2016, he was crushed in this 96 percent Hispanic county, losing 19–79 percent.[23] In 2020, he rallied 55 percent net on margin to narrowly lose Starr County by only 5 percent, with a 47–52 percent split in favor of Biden.[24] In next door Zapata County, an 86 percent Hispanic area, Trump won by 5 percent in 2020, after getting drubbed by 38 percent in 2016.

But the gains do not stop there. Not at all. This trend is not just a Donald Trump phenomenon, nor only a 2020 story. Looking at the returns of the 2022 midterm elections, Ron DeSantis surged to a commanding reelection as governor of Florida. After a narrow 0.4 percent win in 2018, the Governor romped to reelection with

---

23 "2016 Texas Presidential Election Results" (Politico, December 13, 2016), https://www.politico.com/2016-election/results/map/president/texas/.

24 "Live Results: 2020 U.S. Presidential Election" (*People's Pundit Daily*, June 13, 2024) https://www.peoplespunditdaily.com/elections/live-results-2020-us-presidential-election/.

an astounding 19 percent blowout victory in November 2022.[25] That kind of move in just four years is astounding.

What explains this incredible surge?

Well, for starters, DeSantis has transformed Florida from a swing state into a dependably red GOP stronghold through solidly populist conservative governing. DeSantis managed Florida during the pandemic using science instead of fearmongering tactics or tyrannical mandates from Anthony Fauci and other contemptible public health authorities in Washington, DC. DeSantis also confronted woke corporations, such as Disney, when the conglomerate tried to insert itself into state politics to support the sexualized education of young Florida schoolchildren.

Given this backdrop, unsurprisingly, Hispanics in Florida rallied toward their governor. Miami-Dade County is the most populous Latino-majority county in America. Prior to DeSantis, it had become an increasingly Democratic area. In fact, no GOP governor had won Miami-Dade in two decades. DeSantis himself was beaten soundly there in his victorious 2018 election, losing the South Florida population center by a whopping 21 percent. Then, four years later, DeSantis won Miami-Dade by a comfortable 10 percent, totaling a stunning 31 percent net gain in only four years.[26]

The main difference? It was Hispanics, but not only the Republican-leaning Cubans of the Miami area. This Florida data and this performance by DeSantis provide a roadmap for political success across America among Hispanic voters. Overall,

---

25 "Florida Governor Election Results 2018" (Politico, June 13, 2018), https://www.politico.com/election-results/2018/florida/governor/; "Ron DeSantis (R) won the race for Florida Governor" (Politico, November 26, 2023), https://www.politico.com/2022-election/results/florida/statewide-offices/.

26 "Florida Governor Election Results 2022: Live Map" www.politico.com/2022-election/results/florida/statewide-offices/.

the 2022 midterms were very disappointing for the GOP, as the much-ballyhooed red wave became more of a trickle. But Florida stood out as a beacon of what is possible. In fact, DeSantis also showed powerful political coattails, as he lifted every other statewide candidate to victory as well.

For the first time since the Reconstruction Era, every single constitutional office in Florida is now occupied by a Republican—and not just squishy Republicans in name, but bad-ass conservatives who govern like they mean it and use power against the Left with precision and discipline.

These political and economic trends point to much bigger wins ahead for the patriotic populist movement as a prevailing voter bloc in American public life. The marriage of cultural conservatism with economic populist nationalism presents a majority movement that can dominate American politics for decades to come, with Hispanics at the fore of that ascendance.

Specifically, the movement centers on three core principles: restoring sovereignty, resurrecting our culture, and diffusing power via economic populism. On that last point, the concentration of political and economic power in America represents a trend that is not only unfortunate but also threatens the stability of our republic. Conjoined political and economic power so intensifies among a relatively small group of people, in fact, that our country slides materially into oligarchy.

The republic is clearly still savable—we have not lost the capacity for self-governance and an appreciation for constitutional rule—but the clock is clearly ticking as the oligarchs consolidate power.

Concerning diffused economic power, the entrepreneurial acumen and zeal of Hispanic Americans is again a key point of resistance. Only through empowering small businesses again can our country start to break the fused power of the corporatist globalists who act in fascist concert with the permanent political class. Restoring the dynamism of small businesses will encourage a lot of Hispanic entrepreneurs—bad hombres and proud Latinas—to thrive throughout the 2020s.

I count myself among those bad hombres—running my own business, advocating full-time in the media and political realms, and trying to save this great nation. It's been quite a ride for me, and it's far from over. I hope this book will inform and inspire you to join in this epic quest to reclaim America with Hispanics in the lead.

MASCULINITY AND HISPANICS

Will the next Teddy Roosevelt be an American of Latino heritage? Perhaps named something like Tomas Ramirez, the "new TR"? Such a notion would probably shock the real blue-blooded TR, whose ancestors came from the Netherlands over to New York, which was still New Amsterdam at the time.

Roosevelt was a true Renaissance man, despite being transplanted from the Old World to the brave new Continent. He was every bit as adept at boxing as he was at deciphering great literature. He was as skilled with a shotgun as he was with a writing pen. Roosevelt showed steadfast bravery and intense patriotism. He modeled manliness and espoused unabashed, patriotic, American nationalism. Men such as TR have become tragically rare in most American communities today.

So, to save America, American men must lead the way. If we are to reclaim the republic and recapture American greatness, we must reverse the present trends of gender confusion and neutering of men. When I speak of gender confusion, I do not merely mean the obvious absurdity from the Left that pretends a human being can change their innate, God-ordained sex. We on the Right are correctly outraged about such lies, especially when they are leveraged to exploit confused and vulnerable children who make life-altering changes to their bodies through chemical and surgical castrations.

Those affronts to decency and logic shock the consciences of any well-meaning person, of course. But those extreme examples should mostly point to the more mundane decline of masculinity in American life. In our modern culture, the traits of a true man have become not just diminished, but downright denigrated. If we are going to renew a culture that uplifts authentic masculinity again, then Hispanic bad hombres must lead the way.

Until recently, America has long been a particularly masculine nation. That statement will offend the gender confusion activists and the feminists who now dominate most important American institutions of importance. Others would object to that thesis because America has long been, quite rightly, a place that affords equal rights to women in ways unmatched in the rest of the world, especially ancient societies like China and India.

But the reality of American history reveals our country was dominated by a particularly masculine ethos from the earliest days of European settlement. Taming the wild lands of America from Jamestown and Plymouth Rock all the way to the Western frontier required testosterone in abundance, and American men rose to the occasion throughout the glorious history of the republic.

These men found an indispensable support system from the women in their lives—and in society at large—who likewise respected and honored well-directed masculinity. Perhaps the apex of this ideal of American masculinity was found in President Theodore Roosevelt.

The youngest man to ever serve as president, Roosevelt spoke frequently and passionately about the need for motivated, masculine leaders for America—in the home, in communities, and at the national level. His own life exemplified the traits of authentic masculinity, as Roosevelt himself overcame physical maladies as a sickly boy to grow into a man of virility and high adventure. His feats as a hunter and sportsman became legendary, and his bravery on the battlefield fighting for the US Army earned him the coveted Medal of Honor.

In fact, one of the more moving experiences of my political career was my visit to the Roosevelt Room in the West Wing of the White House, where I had the chance to admire his Medal of Honor in person. I confess that until I actually visited the Roosevelt Room for meetings with President Trump and senior staffers, I thought it was only dedicated to Franklin Roosevelt. In fact, that august room pays equal honor to cousins Franklin *and* Theodore Roosevelt. It has been the setting some of the most important decisions in US history, the location of innumerable press question shouting scenes, and a place memorialized in many political TV shows and movies.

On the wall of that room, the mounted Medal of Honor pays tribute to TR, a man who personified masculinity for generations of Americans. He would not be pleased with the state of the sexes in 2020s America to say the least. But he might also find hope and promise among Hispanic men, the best hope from here to lead a regeneration of masculinity in American society.

How important is this issue?

Well, of all the many problems that afflict modern American society, perhaps the single most vexing issue is the diminution of authentic masculinity as an unattainable goal for men. On the parental side, fatherless homes pervade and spread among social, economic, and ethnic demographics of society, including among Latinos.

The consequences of fatherlessness have been nothing short of catastrophic for our country, regardless if the fathers are entirely absent or only partially involved in the lives of their children. Children raised without loving, present fathers fall prey to every possible pathology at higher rates than children raised with fathers, especially if their father is married to their mother. Suicide, teen pregnancy, depression, and incidence of criminality all rise materially as a fallout of fatherless homes.

But even for physically present fathers, the emasculation of men in American society rolls along as a structural and cultural force that is almost unimpeded and unanalyzed, except from small corners of the Christian Right. This derision for men leads, of course, to rudderless and often angry boys becoming unhealthy and even unstable young men who find their masculinity in unproductive ways, such as violence, gang affiliations, substance abuse, or reckless sexual conquests.

As much as the Left longs to fully squash masculinity, the vast majority of boys will eventually recognize their inner, God-ordained manhood and seek to assert it. When properly channeled, such masculinity becomes a driving force for any healthy society; it certainly was for all American history until recently.

But when that masculinity is artificially repressed, as is the norm in America today, it will inevitably rise to the surface. Like trying to keep a beach ball underwater in a pool, the leftists undertake a foolish task. The masculinity will emerge, but it will likely appear in harmful ways rather than as the productive forces of protection and progress our society needs.

Here the massive population of Hispanic men in America could well become the saving grace of American society. Some aspects of Latin culture that are imported into American society are not helpful and should be resisted by legacy Americans as well as by Hispanic newcomers. But the Latin focus on masculinity provides a very welcome addition to modern American culture—and, in fact, a life raft to save a country adrift in malicious feminine propaganda and toxic gender confusion.

This Latin insistence on authentic masculinity does not flow from some stereotypical place of mere machismo, though there is some validity to that inference. For example, part of the allure of President Trump for Latino men has been his strong male characteristics. He is, after all, a man of serious accomplishments and abundant self-confidence, and he possesses the trappings of such qualities, including wealth and a gorgeous wife. There is some mystique among Hispanics for leaders who project strength, acting as the man-on-horseback caudillos of action.

But Hispanic masculinity flows from a much deeper reservoir of thought and servant leadership than caricatured typecasts. Instead, the main focus of this masculinity involves selfless service, especially the protection of the weaker members of a family or society, and the promotion of strength in all endeavors, from work to recreation.

Such traits formerly were the building blocks of American society. But, like so many useful vestiges of prior eras, these ideas have been tossed aside for more "enlightened" mores that actually produce calamity for communities. Once again, as with so many vexing issues in American life, only Hispanics stand ready and capable of providing the antidote here, capable of leading America up and out from this morass of feminism and unisex delusion.

Only Hispanics have the numbers, the culture, and the determination to form a bulwark of a grand renaissance for an ailing America. That reality is broadly true, but especially so regarding sex roles and the need to rebuild a nation that is masculine in its outlook and conduct.

Of course, such ideas are anathema to the androgynous sophisticates of the American ruling class. For the males of this credentialed group, their sex actually serves as a source of shame. Consequently, important men in various positions of power support such cruelties as sex changes for confused children. These so called leaders are men like Joe Biden, prominent religious clergy, and corporate chieftains.

One well known writer who subscribes to these illusions is Eric Garcia, former writer for the *Washington Post*. Garcia wrote successful books that were turned into high profile movies, and he also attended prestigious schools including the University of Southern California and Cornell. As one might expect given that curriculum vitae, Garcia fully embraces the ruling-class sentiments on culture and politics.

Despite his Mexican heritage, Garcia has clearly bought into the dominant left-wing ethos of America—especially that of his former employer, the Jeff Bezos-owned *Washington Post*. Because of this squish worldview, Garcia wrote an in-depth piece for *Washington Post Magazine* bemoaning his father's support for Donald Trump, and he used his frustration as a jumping off point to dive into the larger issue of why Hispanic men aggressively turn politically to the Right.[27]

---

27 Eric Garcia, "Trump, My Dad and the Rightward Shift of Latino Men" (*Washington Post Magazine,* March 22, 2021), https://washingtonpost.com/magazine/2021/03/22/latino-men-trump-2020/.

His father sounds like exactly the kind of masculine bad hombre I describe in these pages. Millions of men like Mr. Garcia can, and will, lead a renaissance of American society. But some of them will also have to endure the criticisms from the establishment that prefers a "brave new world" of gender-neutral softness.

Regarding Trump specifically, Garcia explains how his father represents the macro movements of millions of Latinos. His dad first reviled Trump in 2016. There are important reasons for this initial skepticism among Hispanics toward Trump. First, Trump badly erred with his harsh "rapists and murderers" opening line after coming down the escalator at Trump Tower to announce his run. He was right, of course, to highlight the incredible dangers posed to American citizens.

Every illegal alien crime is completely preventable, and Trump was one of the first national politicians with the guts and vision to expose that reality. Importantly, the primary victims of such crimes are Hispanic citizens of America! In general, dangerous illegal aliens are not hanging around wealthy white enclaves like Greenwich, Connecticut, or McLean, Virginia. Instead, they mostly terrorize the heavily Latino areas of the United States.

Of course, sometimes they do strike in the most surprising of places, such as the horrific slaying of Laken Riley at the University of Georgia. Another shocking example was the brutal shooting death of Kate Steinle on a popular tourist pier in San Francisco. For the most part, however, illegal criminals harass, intimidate, and kill people with last names like Ramirez, Soriano, and Cortes.

So Trump was right to point out this totally preventable risk, but he was wrong in tactics. He voluntary handed over a powerful talking point to his opposition—the myth that Trump hates Latinos. As a side note here, I want to share what President Trump said to me the first time I entered the Oval Office in March 2017. He immediately asked what he could do to help Hispanic citizens of this country. No cameras, only a few people in the room, and that question came foremost to his mind upon welcoming me into the inner chamber of American political power. If he had been more judicious with his words in the summer of 2015 after coming down the escalator, that version of Trump would have been an easier sell with Latinos.

But the second aspect of initial Hispanic antipathy for Trump was a force that resided outside of his control—the totally corrupt corporate media. At first, the media actually gave Trump reasonably balanced press coverage. After all, they loved the ratings and clickbait gold of a bona-fide TV celebrity running for president. With Trump's charisma and personality—and his masculinity—he made for terrific copy and fantastic videos. In addition, they did not really take him seriously, assuming that the GOP establishment would eventually prevail and end his entertaining but unserious run for the presidency.

Of course, that tone changed dramatically once it became clear that Trump was not just seriously competing for the 2016 nomination but was in fact the front-runner. Perhaps most emblematic of this shift is the MSNBC daily kickoff show, *Morning Joe*. Joe Scarborough and Mika Brzezinski lavished airtime and praise on candidate Trump from the early days of the Republican primary all the way through Trump's triumph in the 2016 New Hampshire primary. In fact, they could not get enough of "the Donald" with call-ins to their show every couple days.

Those of us on the campaign were incredulous at just how starry-eyed those hosts were, especially Mika, who basically openly flirted with Trump on live television. As for Joe, few will remember this occurrence, but Trump actually thanked him from the podium after winning the New Hampshire primary. How often does a GOP primary candidate publicly thank a mainstream media host?

But once Trump marched toward the nomination, and once he sharpened and focused his populist nationalist messaging agenda, *Morning Joe* and the rest of the corporate media turned on him with reckless abandon. A large part of their attacks centered around his supposed prejudice against Hispanic citizens of the United States.

Of course, Joe and Mika quickly switched sides and transformed into the lathering leaders of the most unhinged anti-Trump media zealots. Their show reversed completely, morphing into a daily morning show of emotional and unrestrained Trump hatred. That new, propagandist stance continues to this day. This reversal is particularly remarkable for Joe, who was a reasonably conservative congressman from the Florida panhandle. Completely forsaking that past record, he now talks and bloviates like he's on the faculty at Brown University—just without any of the intellectual credentials. On that point, by the way, why is the show named *Morning Joe*? Clearly his wife and co-host Mika is a better broadcaster, and she is immensely smarter than the dense and predictable Joe. It should be named *Morning Mika*.

But back in 2016, that show joined in a broad media assault on Trump that relied heavily on the ridiculous premise that he and his supporters were bigots. Though totally unfounded, of course, this constant stream of narrative promotion gravely harmed Trump's cause among Hispanics. The dishonest narrative attacks were especially virulent on Spanish-language platforms, with charlatans like Jorge Ramos, the anchor at Univision, leading the brazenly partisan effort to slander Trump and poison the political well for him among Hispanics.

Regarding Spanish-language media, a lot of non-Spanish speakers, including Hispanic voters, probably have no idea just how awful and partisan those major platforms are. Telemundo and Univision make CNN look ideologically reasonable. This unfortunate reality persists to this day. Some efforts are afoot to provide right-leaning, or at least balanced, Spanish-language news programming, but so far the Spanish media landscape in the United States is still dominated by hardcore left-wing activists. In 2016, when Trump was still brand-new on the political scene, those tilted and illogical attacks on Trump mattered, and they definitely suppressed his support among Latinos.

One of those Latinos, it appears, was the father of Eric Garcia, as explained in his *Washington Post Magazine* piece. Eric states that his father placed Trump as seventeenth out of the large field of seventeen candidates in the 2016 Republican primary. Once Trump secured the nomination, Eric's father nonetheless pledged to "hold my nose and vote for Trump."[28]

Then Trump took office and everything changed not just for Mr. Garcia, but for millions of Garcias across America. Trump displayed strong masculinity in office, appealing with great success to bad hombres across the land. But even more importantly, he governed as a determined businessman with a populist America First worldview.

The results were outstanding, and especially so for Hispanics. For example, blue-collar laborers shot to the lead in income gains. Most Hispanics fit into this category because we are not generally a high-income community. Not yet at least! But Trump's policies

---

[28] Ibid.

lifted real wages for all income brackets, most markedly those of blue-collar laborers. Incidentally, this topic of real wages versus nominal wages is crucial. Real wages are adjusted for inflation—take-home pay versus the costs of the goods and services you need to live.

Under Trump, real wages soared, particularly in 2019, which was a golden year for the success of MAGAnomics. 2019 was, by many measures, the best year in US history for workers, and Hispanics benefited disproportionately to the upside. This surge in real wages contrasts directly with Joe Biden's administration. Under the failure of Bidenomics, real wages have plunged as his runaway inflation devours any pay increases workers have seen. The net reality? Masses of US laborers, many of them brown citizens, are working harder to get poorer. This is the exact opposite of the economic success of Trump's era, especially for Latinos.

Looking back to those salad days, Hispanic support for Trump unsurprisingly blossomed. This trend was especially evident among Hispanic men like Eric's dad. Not only did he not "hold his nose" in 2020 when he voted for Trump, he "voted while breathing through his nose as clearly as somebody could when wearing a face mask."[29]

Note the face mask reference there, incidentally. Unscientific and unreasonable insistence on masking became a political and cultural sacrament for the Left. But that absurdity aside, the important point here is the complete transformation of bad hombres across the land from either Trump-opposing or Trump-hesitant supporters into full-throated Trump enthusiasts. This shift is what propelled Trump to shock the political world with

---

[29] Ibid.

his 38 percent share of the Hispanic vote, per Pew Research Center's "validated voter" survey.[30]

Some of these newfound Trump enthusiasts had long been Republicans, but they became very different conservatives as a result of the populist movement. I am one of those people. I had been basically a Wall Street Republican prior to 2016. But the Tea Party movement planted seeds of political change in my mind, especially as I was troubled by the massive bank bailouts. Mega cap corporations got lavish benefits and near total absolution from the lies, excesses, and mistakes of the Great Recession, but regular homeowners got the shaft. There was no such benevolence or benefit for upside-down homeowners facing eviction, ruined credit, and financial agony.

Those seeds of doubt in my mind grew into full-fledged populism with the arrival of Donald Trump on the national political scene. When he derided so-called free trade as a gift to massive multinationals and outsourcing initiatives, I became a true convert. I knew from my career and intense study of global economics that "free trade" was a myth anyway. Global trade was completely managed, and it mostly operated for the aggrandizement of the already successful to the detriment of the working-class masses.

Along that same line of thinking, when Trump properly assailed China for its abuses of American workers, he won me over and millions of like-minded bad hombres like Garcia, too, who declared that other GOP presidents "can't compare with what Trump has done."[31] He further described Trump as "brilliant…he is just a master."[32]

---

30 Shepard, "New poll shows how Trump surged with women and Hispanics—and lost anyway."

31 Garcia, "Trump, My Dad and the Rightward Shift of Latino Men."

32 Ibid.

In the *Washington Post Magazine* piece, Eric Garcia explains just how astounding the Hispanic move to the political Right was from 2016 to 2020. The *Washington Post* uses its own exit polling numbers, plus some from CNN. Exit polling can be problematic, so I much prefer the Pew Research Center's "validated voter" survey. Even better, in highly Hispanic geographies, just use the actual vote returns, of course! But even if you accept the data of the *Post*, though it underplays the extent of the rightward shift, the moves are still staggering and hopeful for the populist nationalist movement among Hispanics.

For example, the *Washington Post* concedes that Trump only lost Florida Hispanics by 5 percent in 2020 after losing them by a whopping 27 percent in 2016.[33] Right after the 2020 election cycle, Governor Ron DeSantis built on that rightward Hispanic trend in his own gubernatorial reelection. In fact, DeSantis won the Hispanic vote statewide, in a former swing state, by a stunning 19 percent. This was a key element of his romp to reelection. Looking at the details of the DeSantis triumph, his gains in Florida's largest county, Miami-Dade, were astounding. In this heavily Hispanic, urban-suburban metro area, DeSantis swung from a 20 percent deficit in 2018 to a 9 percent win in 2022. Amazing—and fueled by Hispanics.[34]

These kinds of Trump and DeSantis moves that occurred in just four years are astounding, especially for a large population like Florida Latinos. For the most part, macro shifts in politics take several election cycles. But this shift of Latinos to the

---

[33] Ibid.

[34] Katherine Fung, "Ron DeSantis Wins Over Hispanic County That Rejected Him in 2018 Election" (*Newsweek*, November 8, 2022), https://www.newsweek.com/ron-desantis-2022-midterm-election-wins-miami-dade-county-which-rejected-him-2018-1758069.

Right happened in the blink of an eye. In fact, Hispanics have formed the core of the movement to the New Right—and among Hispanics, men comprise the lead.

One of the most impressive statistics of all flows from key battleground state North Carolina, where Trump narrowly won in 2020. One of the unheralded reasons he took the Tar Heel State? He won Hispanic men by a runaway 20 percent, even though he lost Latina women by 54 percent.[35] That kind of disparity is a unicorn in politics. Similarly, in Nevada, Trump won Hispanic men by 6 percent but lost Hispanic women by 47 percent.[36]

The biggest driving forces for those men toward Trump were his masculinity and the success of his economic agenda. On the first point about style and culture, his worldview simply matched far better with Latino men than the effeminate, globalist, and limp outlook of the 2020s Democrats. For example, activists, academics, and even Democrat politicians embrace the ridiculous phrase Latinx to replace Latino, since the latter is masculine tense.

Never mind that these language colonists want to alter the centuries-old Spanish language to fit their twenty-first century Marxist worldview. These radicals also expect normal, hard-working Hispanics to change their very language to assuage a tiny fringe of the Chicano Studies Department at the University of California at Berkeley. On this topic, another big Latino sex disparity emerges. Among young Latinas aged eighteen to twenty-nine years old, 14 percent of those women actually welcome

[35] Garcia, "Trump, My Dad and the Rightward Shift of Latino Men."
[36] Ibid.

the term Latinx. But among young men of the same age, a scant 1 percent do, according to the Pew Research Center.[37]

Hispanic men also rally to the America First movement because they have a large and growing population working in law enforcement. For example, Customs and Border Protection is the most Hispanic agency of the entire federal government.[38] Hispanic men working as police officers across America vaults higher, doubling in the last decade. [39]

Now, not every Hispanic who works in law enforcement is right-leaning, but most are. For example, in a national study of policemen regarding police shootings of black suspects, Hispanic officers concurred with white policemen, with 72 percent of them determining that police killings of black suspects were not indicative of any systemic police problem.[40] In contrast, nearly half of black police officers said there was a systemic problem.

Modern Democrats are increasingly becoming the party that not only tolerates reckless lawlessness but actually celebrates it. Consider, for example, the full-on embrace and near-deification of George Floyd and the 2020 riots that ensued after his death. Whether or not the police acted properly in subduing the

---

[37] Luis Noe-Bustamante, Lauren Mora, and Mark Hugo Lopez, "About One-in-Four U.S. Hispanics Have Heard of Latinx, but Just 3% Use It" (Pew Research Center, August 11, 2020), https://www.pewresearch.org/race-and-ethnicity/2020/08/11/about-one-in-four-u-s-hispanics-have-heard-of-latinx-but-just-3-use-it/.

[38] Anna Giaritelli, "Hispanic Agents Make Up Majority of Border Patrol Yet White Men Dominate Leadership Posts," August 5, 2022, washingtonexaminer.com/news/1188606/Hispanic-agents-make-up-majority-of-border-patrol-yet-white-men-dominate-leadership-posts/.

[39] Israel Duro, "Hispanic Representation Increases in Law Enforcement," May 14, 2024, voz.us/en/society/240514/10360/Hispanic-representation-increases-in-law-enforcement.html.

[40] Rich Morin et al., "Police, fatal encounters and ensuing protests" (Pew Research Center, January 11, 2017), https://www.pewresearch.org/social-trends/2017/01/11/police-fatal-encounters-and-ensuing-protests/.

uncooperative Floyd, this man lived a life of criminality and disrepute. He was a derelict who should not be honored by any reasonable person, and certainly not by leaders with political power. Yet the Left saw a political opportunity and literally erected statues to honor this convicted felon who brought so much misery to those around him for decades.

That kind of cognitive dissonance does not play well with Hispanics broadly, and especially not with bad hombre Hispanic men. But the entire ruling class accepted the summer 2020 riots as somehow noble—even facilitating them in many cases. For example, then-Senator Kamala Harris used her large media platform to raise money for the so-called Minnesota Freedom Fund, which raised money to post bail for violent offenders who were arrested during the destructive post-Floyd riots in the Twin Cities.[41] Among those who Kamala helped to release was an assailant charged with the attempted murder of police officers.

That kind of radicalism simply does not play in the American Hispanic community, and especially not among men. While Vice President Harris now lives a life of luxury and around-the-clock Secret Service protection that we taxpayers provide, regular Americans have to live with the consequences of her pro-crime agenda. Similarly, while she cashes large taxpayer-funded paychecks, working-class Hispanic citizens must compete in the labor market against illegal workers who Harris invited in by the

---

41 Kamala Harris (@KamalaHarris), "If you're able to, chip in now to the @MNFreedomFund to help post bail for those protesting on the ground in Minnesota" (X, June 1, 2020), https://x.com/KamalaHarris/status/1267555018128965643?ref_src=twsrc%5Etfw%7Ctwcamp%5Etweetembed%7Ctwterm%5E1267555018128965643%7Ctwgr%5E36919c473a3fb641443055e31b35c23740b00bdb%7Ctwcon%5Es1_&ref_url=https%3A%2F%2Fwww.foxnews.com%2Fpolitics%2Fminnesota-bail-fund-promoted-kamala-harris-freed-convict-now-charged-murder.

millions. These kinds of contrasts and disparities push Hispanics ever more to the Right.

One such Hispanic is my amigo Tommy Vallejos. I first met Tommy at the White House at a Cinco de Mayo party. Those gatherings during Trump's tenure were a blast. We Hispanics know how to have fun, and the music, tacos, comradery, and laughter of the White House Hispanic fiestas were a wonderful gift to me and the hundreds of Hispanic leaders who were honored to attend these gatherings.

Meeting people like Tommy was an added bonus, and we started really working together once I moved to his state of Tennessee. Tommy is extremely active in Latinos for Tennessee, a non-partisan advocacy organization, and he also participates in partisan GOP politics, serving as a county commissioner and running for the state legislature. But perhaps most impressive about Tommy is his ministry work with Men of Valor, an incredible program for incarcerated and recently released convicts. More on that amazing organization below, but first a look into the life of one bad hombre, Tommy Vallejos.

Long before Tommy became the first Hispanic elected to any county commission in the state of Tennessee, he lived through tough times.[42] Through both his circumstances and his poor personal choices, his early years were the epitome of the thug life.

In fact, as a boy and young man in New Mexico, Tommy could be accurately described as a pachuco—a violent gang member who willingly engaged in brutal turf battles. One of nine

[42] Patricia Vélez Santiago, "From gang member to politician: the story of Tennessee's first Hispanic commissioner" (Univision News, October 12, 2016), https://www.univision.com/univision-news/from-gang-member-to-politician-the-story-of-tennessees-first-hispanic-commissioner.

children, Tommy became a tough criminal soldier alongside his brothers before the US military would make him a real soldier.

As a young man, he lost two of his brothers to gang violence. He became intent on avenging their deaths, even shooting a man in a wild melee with other pachucos who were hell-bent on killing him to erase a third brother of the family. Thankfully Tommy's bullets did not kill anyone, but the violence compelled his mother to ship him out of state to Texas for safety. She forbade Tommy to return to New Mexico for a full year after.

Tommy's early life represents the worst aspects of masculinity. When a young man's innate nature is not properly formed and directed, it leads to the most pernicious manifestations of masculinity. He grew up without a father and often turned to the tough streets of a New Mexico barrio for misdirected guidance.

As stated earlier, that suppressed beachball of masculine energy is not staying underwater; it will pop up somewhere. Often, when not properly harnessed toward the good—through faith, sports, and male mentorship—that manly spirit becomes a propellant of carnage.

So Tommy was living the unfortunate reality of a "toxic masculinity"—but not in the way the Left would have us believe. They see authentic masculinity itself as toxic—a powerful method used by the ruling class to suppress real men, create anger among boys, and foster gender confusion anxiety. But there is such a thing as toxic masculinity, as modeled by the mistakes and sins of Tommy in his early life. Masculinity that is perverted toward cruelty and power distorts the true potential of laudable masculinity that leads, creates, and protects.

His road upward from the depths of a dangerous and unproductive life started with the military. Like many Mexican

Americans, Tommy saw the army as his only route out of a life of depravity. In the military, his toughness found the proper channel and became useful for a country he loved despite his poor track record of behavior. In fact, he admitted to me that even in the military, while he improved dramatically as a citizen, he still secretly engaged in criminal activities on the side like drug dealing.

But the Holy Spirit was at work in Tommy's life, gnawing at him to be a better husband and father to his young family. He performed admirably as a soldier and was stationed all over the world, including deployments to the first Gulf War, Germany, and South Korea. It was in Korea that he was saved and gave his mind, heart, and soul over to Jesus Christ. Tommy had a dream one night and discerned the call of God to conversion. With this conversion, his transformation was complete, and he left all vestiges of the destructive life he knew before.

His last army post brought him to Fort Campbell and a home in Clarksville, Tennessee. Before leaving the military, Tommy became a minister and dedicated community leader. His hardscrabble cholo past is still evident by his neck tattoos and scars from brawls. However, he grew into a man of servant leadership, compassion, and deep patriotism, and he still is to this day.

Along with his close friend and colleague, Raul Lopez, Tommy gave much of his new life to service through Men of Valor. This Christian prison ministry group operates across Tennessee providing both tangible instructions and Christian witness to jailed men and those recently released. The ministry members teach practical skills, provide post-release supervised housing, and serve as mentors and faith-filled father figures to convicts in need of personal restoration.

Raul Lopez has a very different story from Tommy. Raul's family came to America from Cuba. On paper, Raul and Tommy do not have much in common except for heritage tracing to Latin America. But in America, these Hispanics find common cause, especially because of their shared faith in Christ. But regardless of spiritual status, Hispanics like Raul and Tommy represent the best chance to save America. These two represent the best of American men. They are masculine, proudly conservative, faith-filled, and selflessly focused on service of God and country.

These kinds of men with these traits were formerly common in America, especially in positions of influence. But now they are too sparse. In this regard, Hispanic men are best positioned to lead a national renewal because the Hispanic population has not, on the whole, relinquished the immutable truths about the complementarity and excess of the two sexes.

In addition to their realism regarding sex roles and their embrace of authentic masculinity, Hispanics also rally to ideals of proud patriotism. In far too many segments of American society, patriotism becomes verboten. Love of country is largely regarded as retrograde among the managerial elites. Among black Americans, a corrupt leadership cadre has fully succumbed to a victim mentality, securing the outsize benefits that flow to shady blacks of influence like Al Sharpton and Jesse Jackson. Consequently, the burden of leadership for an American renaissance mostly falls upon Hispanics, and especially upon Hispanic men.

Such leadership cannot be properly exercised without the correct understanding and elevation of authentic masculinity. In particular ways, Hispanics stand ready to serve as the saving heroes of America. But such a Latino-led renewal will not just unfold by chance. Instead, that restoration requires a volitional decision to serve as the bulwark of a great national renewal. This can only occur if Hispanics are willing to speak hard truths about the problems facing our society and the available paths to escape them.

Confronting this great challenge, new Hispanic versions of Teddy Roosevelt bad hombres rise up across the country. Their ascendance is political in part, but they play an even bigger role in leadership at the household, community, and national levels.

ENTREPRENEURSHIP

Bad hombres rally to the America First movement in large measure because it promotes broader economic success by enabling small businesses to thrive. In this regard, the unmatched entrepreneurial zeal of Hispanics provides an indispensable foundation to America's overall renewal.

Hispanics embrace entrepreneurship like no other group in America. For example, according to the Joint Economic Committee of the US Senate, in the decade prior to the pandemic, the number of Hispanic business owners increased by a whopping 34 percent.[43] The overall number for the rest of the US population was a scant 1 percent increase. Not only are the amounts of new Hispanic businesses increasing, but they also enjoy a torrid rate of revenue growth.[44] In fact, according to the

---

[43] Don Beyer, "Hispanic Entrepreneurs and Businesses Are Helping to Drive the Economy's Entrepreneurial Growth and Job Creation" (Joint Economic Committee, November 4, 2021), https://www.jec.senate.gov/public/index.cfm/democrats/2021/11/hispanic-entrepreneurs-and-businesses-are-helping-to-drive-the-economy-s-entrepreneurial-growth-and-job-creation.

[44] Steve Cortes and Javier Palomarez, "Hispanic Entrepreneurs Need Tax Reform" (*Wall Street Journal: Opinion*, December 10, 2017), https://www.wsj.com/articles/hispanic-entrepreneurs-need-tax-reform-1512938597.

Hispanic Chamber of Commerce, Hispanic firms grow at twice the rate of US companies overall.

Our community simply loves to start new ventures. Why? Well, for starters, Hispanics promote a culture of work. As for the bad hombres, Hispanic men boast the highest workforce participation rate of any group in America—and by a lot. According to the Department of Labor, 75 percent of all Latino males were in the workforce in 2021. For comparison, that number is 66 percent for white males and 60 percent for black men.[45]

Of course, the economic ambition is not only the provenance of the bad hombres. In some respects, the proud Latina ladies of America start to even outshine their male compadres. For example, a post-COVID-19 survey from Spanish-language broadcaster Telemundo found that a stunning 20 percent of all Hispanic women plan to open a new business in the next few years, far above the rate of non-Hispanic women. In the last fifteen years, the number of Latina-owned businesses has nearly doubled, rocketing to over two million firms—more than an 87 percent increase.[46]

Whether men or women (and yes, we Hispanics believe in a grand total of two sexes), Hispanics are twice as likely as other Americans to start new businesses.[47]

---

45 U.S. Bureau of Labor Statistics, "Labor force characteristics by race and ethnicity, 2021" (BLS Reports, January 2023), https://www.bls.gov/opub/reports/race-and-ethnicity/2021/home.htm#:~:text=%2C%20and%205A.)-,Among%20adult%20men%20(20%20years%20and%20older)%20in%20the%20largest,continuing%20a%20longstanding%20employment%20pattern.

46 Patricia Guadalupe, "How female Hispanic business owners are fueling the economy" (Legal Zoom, November 8, 2023), https://www.legalzoom.com/articles/how-female-hispanic-business-owners-are-fueling-the-economy.

47 Bertha Coombs, "Latino Americans are twice as likely as other groups to start their own businesses" (CNBN: Closing Bell, October 6, 2021), https://www.cnbc.com/video/2021/10/06/latino-americans-are-twice-as-likely-as-other-groups-to-start-their-own-businesses.html.

Other than a commitment to hard work, what explains this orientation?

I am convinced that a large part of this culture of entrepreneurship flows, paradoxically, from the lack of small business dynamism in Latin America. Unfortunately, our ancestral homelands from Mexico down to Argentina have been weighed down by stifling economic statism and stagnation. The mores and regulations of most of Latin America dissuade or preclude entrepreneurship. One major example is Mexico's total state control of all-natural resources, especially oil. When entire industries must solely answer to central government authorities, innovation is choked off and crony corruption thrives.

Consequently, Hispanic Americans who come to this country carry with them a burning desire to forge an entirely different economic path. Even for the children and grandchildren of such immigrants, this characteristic zeal is passed down as an aspirational goal and even as a sort of challenge. This predilection for start-ups represents a corollary to the fervent anti-communism of Cuban Americans. In other words, just as the Cubans who fled to America despise the communism of their homeland, the bad hombre entrepreneurs of America want no part in Mexican or Argentine-style economic statism.

Given this wholesale embrace of start-up culture and the vibrancy of the Hispanic economy in America, Latinos naturally gravitate rightward to a philosophical and political cause that promises both opportunity and protection. On the opportunity side, one only needs to look at the pre-pandemic results of President Trump's first term to ascertain how massively entrepreneurs and working-class people benefit from populist nationalist economic policies.

In fact, 2019 unfolded as a true golden year for American workers; it was arguably the best year in US history for wage earners. President Trump unleashed the full power of American domestic energy production—a sector with a sizable share of Latinos in the workforce. In addition, the historic tax and regulatory relief ignited a boom for Main Street, for start-ups, and for regular laborers. For example, wage growth exceeded 3 percent in every single month of 2019 with minimal inflation, so real incomes expanded materially, meaning pay adjusted for the cost of living.[48] For the lowest 10 percent of earners, wages jumped an astonishing 7 percent in 2019.[49] This cohort, by definition, includes many Hispanics. Similarly, the wage gains for working-class citizens without a high school diploma leapt higher by 9 percent.

Populist economic policies proved overall efficacy at growing prosperity, and particularly so for those left behind during the Obama-Biden years. That administration ushered in an unprecedented concentration of wealth among only the credentialed elites, almost none of whom are Hispanic. Specifically, according to Federal Reserve data, during the eight years of Obama-Biden, only the top 10 percent of earners saw their net worth increase.[50] The rest of the country—the masses that comprise the 90 percent—saw their net worth decline for almost a decade. Such

---

[48] Steve Cortes, "Trump's Top 10 Achievements for 2019" (*Real Clear Politics*, December 31, 2019), https://www.realclearpolitics.com/articles/2019/12/31/trumps_top_10_achievements_for_2019_142047.html.

[49] Gary D. Cohn and Kevin Hassett, "Tax Reform Has Delivered for Workers" (*Wall Street Journal: Opinion*, December 22, 2019), https://www.wsj.com/articles/tax-reform-has-delivered-for-workers-11577045463?ns=prod/accounts-wsj.

[50] "2022 Survey of Consumer Finances" (Board of Governors of the Federal Reserve System, 2023), https://www.federalreserve.gov/econres/scfindex.htm.

widespread economic failure had not been inflicted in America since the Great Depression.

So the supposed progressives produced unparalleled economic inequality while the populists created the conditions for broad prosperity. If that incredible economic ascent had not been artificially halted by the ravages of COVID-19 and the concomitant, insane overreactions of government and media across America, imagine how much more momentum working-class people would enjoy today!

But of course, the economic damage at this point is spilled milk, and there is no way to rewind the clock to force the CCP to act honorably or convince state and federal authorities to treat the virus rationally. But, from here forward, we can choose our economic agenda, and the lessons from pre-pandemic prosperity should provide enormous confidence in the efficacy of our economic vision.

As a slight aside here, much of my economic analysis focuses on producing the environment for a flourishing middle class, empowering the aspirational strivers of America. Why? It's not just some nostalgic sentimentality for the great American middle class. Rather, this focus flows from a recognition that the globalist corporatists have been at war with the American middle class for decades. The oligarchs and their allies—in Washington corridors of power and in New York newsrooms—have successfully gutted the masses of formerly prosperous workers for the selfish aggrandizement of a connected, ruling class club of the few.

This destruction of the ambitious strivers of America guts the very fabric of civic society and renders the continuation of a democratic republic impossible. Instead of a nation of shopkeepers, America devolves into a quasi-county ruled by oligarchs with fascistic collaborators in favored private sector operations. These selected winners make up the titans of Silicon Valley Big Tech and the media mavens of Madison Avenue. In return for dutiful compliance with the wishes of the oligarchs, such approved enterprises are showered with the massive accoutrements of acting as the selected organs of the ruling class, resulting in every more concentrated power and the descent of economic and societal dynamism.

As such, the patriotic populist movement stands against this present fascistic trend. This muscular vision of politics champions an agenda that empowers and rewards the working classes on policies that create broad, dispersed success. But this dispersion of economic might unfolds not in the direction of central authority, as prescribed by the populist Left, but rather by creating the conditions for Main Street and entrepreneurs to thrive.

As shown by the statistics and realities described in this book, strategies that help the working classes of America and pave the wave for entrepreneurial success are, by definition, accretive to Hispanics. Why? Because Hispanics are so disproportionately represented among both the overall masses of working-class citizens as well as among the legions of entrepreneurs that power America's economic promise. Helping the "little guy" and the start-up striver inevitably results in a lot of brown guys doing well in life and rising to places of prominence in our society.

Accordingly, an intentional focus on policies that augment the well-being of Hispanic Americans will naturally lead to better lives for all Americans, because enervating small business and restoring a large, prolific middle class will create a country of abundance and stability. In contrast, the present bifurcated society we live in risks a rapid decline into a Third World-like binary.

Our country increasingly operates within a tenuous and volatile bargain where the oligarchs amass all the power and resources and bestow just enough largesse upon the dispossessed masses to placate them. For now.

But that sad reality does not comport with centuries of an American republic that established a society built on firmer foundations than crass, macro bribes. We must restore a country of broad, diffused prosperity that funds families, churches, and communities dedicated to traditional values and the highest aspirations of Western Civilization.

This glorious inheritance has been stolen from the citizens of this country by the connected few. But these godless globalists have pushed their advantages too far, resulting in the populist pushback. A major facet of retaking control of our republic and reenergizing civic society involves spreading prosperity far and wide and breaking down the structures that protect the current elites. Those structures involve both domestic and international politics.

Accordingly, to fully provide the opportunity agenda promised by the new movement, the crucial power of government must stand ready to aggressively act to protect the interests and prerogatives of American citizens. The days of limited government conservatism are over. That ship has sailed.

Theoretically, in a well-functioning society that agrees on first principles and generally operates according to Judeo-Christian values, the smallest possible federal government makes sense. This reality prevailed for much of American history with fantastic benefits. But we do not live in that world anymore. A small, restrained national government cannot remotely smash the powers that presently punish the masses nor stand up against pernicious quasi-government forces that aggressively destroy the building blocks of society. Multinational corporations today, for example, possess levels of market dominance and societal power that dwarf anything seen during the so-called robber baron era. The present economic, political, and social power of firms like Amazon and Google make previously-targeted trusts like AT&T and Standard Oil seem like quaint corner stores.

In addition, the constant assault on America's prosperity from the Chinese Communist Party presents an unprecedented threat that has eviscerated America's industries and communities for decades. This gutting by the CCP only works with the full complicity of an entitled elite, though. Tragically, some of the supposed "best and brightest" of America gleefully submit to the CCP, from leaders of universities and CEOs to the top lobbyists of Washington's corrupt K Street corridor of glad-handers. In return for their submission, the CCP rewards such charlatans mightily. Just consider, for example, the immense power and wealth of Larry Fink, CEO of BlackRock.

Fink is always and everywhere a supplicant for the CCP, defending China's tactics in America media, lobbying on behalf of China's priorities before our elected officials, and actively investing billions of dollars from hardworking US citizens into the direct or indirect enterprises of the deadly Beijing regime. Amazingly, most Americans are unaware just how much of their capital flows to support the Chinese via retirement funds like 401(k)s and other managed money. Even when such funds are not actually invested in China, they still flow to companies fully on board with China's asymmetric trade policies that abuse America at every turn.

The American working classes pay a heavy price for China's predatory trade abuses of the United States. The total lack of fairness and reciprocity in that abusive trade relationship provides foundational proof that we increasingly do not live in a real republic. Moreover, the legacy Republican Party, especially permanent Washington maneuverers like Senator Mitch McConnell, plays right along with the grand con perpetrated by the Chinese Communist Party. In McConnell's case, he likely has material, personal conflicts of interest that further blind him to the economic abuses the CCP heaps upon America.

According to the Economic Policy Institute, a left-leaning think tank, the United States has lost a stunning 3.7 million manufacturing jobs directly to China since Beijing was admitted to the World Trade Organization in 2001.[51] That inclusion for the CCP was a massive gift to the world's most treacherous regimes, one that systemically brutalizes its own people. But the bipartisan permanent political class in Washington saw an opportunity in catering to the CCP junta despite the gargantuan costs to Americans.

Again, these issues matter to all Americans, especially the non-wealthy. But they matter disproportionately to Hispanics. Right now in America, Hispanic citizens are overwhelmingly working-class people and occupy the vanguard of small business creation. As such, these globalists policies that so harm Main Street inflict particular pain upon Hispanics. Consequently, Hispanics must rush to lead the demand for better policies of economic nationalism and protection. Even more, I foresee Hispanics as not

---

[51] Robert E. Scott and Zane Mokhiber, "Growing China trade deficit cost 3.7 million American jobs between 2001 and 2018" (Economic Policy Institute, January 30, 2020), https://www.epi.org/publication/growing-china-trade-deficits-costs-us-jobs/.

only stopping the madness of globalist policies, but also providing the grit and entrepreneurial solutions to fix this mess.

In order to realize those solutions, then, we must fully embrace and promote protectionism. For almost a century, protectionism has been treated as a dirty word within establishment circles, especially among old-school Republicans. But the ghost of Smoot Hawley should no longer scare right-wingers from taking a dispassionate look at the economic policies of the twenty-first century to determine what best serves the interests of American citizens and industries.

First, looking at US firms, does the present concentration of market share and corporate political power promote a truly competitive, capitalist economy? The clear answer into the 2020s is no. As famed economist Milton Freidman famously stated in the 1970s, America should not confuse being pro-free enterprise with being pro-business. In fact, Milton Friedman warned that big businesses usually "have been a major force in undermining the free enterprise system."[52] In this regard, Hispanics really have a dog in the fight. Latinos by and large do not occupy positions of power in the existing, dominant firms, but instead provide the sweat, grit, and smarts of the upstarts.

Indeed, these behemoth multinational giants, especially in tech, presently exploit their scale and overbearing control over consumers to co-opt Washington. These oligopolies then use that huge political leverage to erect massive barriers to entry, precluding serious competition. They aggressively engage in rent-seeking

---

[52] Veronique de Rugy, "The Government Should Be Pro-Market, Not 'Pro-Business'" (Reason Foundation, September 29, 2022), https://reason.com/2022/09/29/the-government-should-be-pro-market-not-pro-business/#:~:text=As%20usual%2C%20Nobel%20Prize%2Dwinning,special%20government%20protection%20for%20himself

activities to augment their market dominance and feed at the taxpayer-funded trough for giant government contracts.

Many examples involve the defense and intelligence communities of the federal government. Giant Silicon Valley firms secure huge vendor contracts for the three-letter agencies of the national security apparatus. In return, these tech firms gladly act as censors and narrative promoters for the Intelligence Community. The most egregious example was the collusion—yes, actual collusion—of the Intelligence Community with Big Tech to successfully bury the most explosive story of the entire 2020 presidential election: "big guy" Joe Biden securing millions of dollars from the most sinister enemies of America through his son Hunter, acting as a bagman for the Biden cartel scam.

So, from both an economic and a political rights perspective, the power and reach of these firms must be restrained. To ignore this task does not serve the interests of free enterprise. Instead, government inaction further erodes and destroys the animal spirits of a truly competitive, free enterprise society.

Looking at this agenda of protectionism through the lens of foreign threats, America must realize that only bullies respond to the credible threat of responsive force. In the case of China, the CCP will continue to exploit and abuse America's acquiescence as long as they are able.

But the America First movement proves that China will bend when forced, seen in the important first steps taken by President Trump in January 2020 to negotiate new trade deals with China. This deal resulted in little tangible benefit for America, unfortunately, because within weeks the global economy began shutting down in a massive overreaction to the pandemic.

Nonetheless, our current trade showdown provides a template for further necessary confrontations with the CCP. America needs significant punitive tariffs as part of a broader, macro decoupling from the criminals of the Beijing Politburo. Our economies are so deeply intertwined that it will take years to shift supply chains away from China and back to the United States or friendly allies. But despite this regrettable reality, the task must begin and once it does, Hispanic Americans will benefit disproportionately.

Every activist on the Right needs to eschew the establishment republican orthodoxy regarding antitrust and so-called free trade. On trust-busting, we must instead channel the approach of one of the greatest Republicans in history, President Teddy Roosevelt. On trade, recognize that "free trade" was always a chimera. We never had free trade. It was always managed by powerful interests, both at home and abroad, and nearly always managed against the interests of American workers and US entrepreneurs...many of them bad hombres.

This approach of economic populism presents the best chance of restoring an American economy of broadly dispersed prosperity. It also returns economic power back to regular citizens and small businesses, thereby providing the incentives for a return to an American culture of work and hustle.

In recent decades, far too many able-bodied Americans have retreated from an economically productive life. The trend was massively exacerbated during the lockdowns, given the huge incentives for the dispossessed and unmotivated to accept taxpayer transfers in lieu of productive work.

Here, Hispanic citizens can lead the way for the rest of America as the country's youngest and hardest-working population group.

But economic populism is not just good policy; it is also good politics. These principles and reforms are immensely popular among citizens and motivating to voters. This new approach especially proves effective at galvanizing Hispanic voters who were previously taken for granted by the statist Democrats and now turn toward unapologetically populist, conservative candidates. This introduction cited huge gains for patriotic populism among Hispanic voters in south Texas and in Florida. Those themes have garnered a reasonable amount of attention, at least within professional political circles. But what about in New York? More specifically, how many Americans are aware of the tectonic political shift to the Right among the Hispanics of formerly deeply-blue New York City?

Looking at the most recent 2022 election in the Big Apple, the trends are just stunning. For example, in New York City in 2018, Governor Andrew Cuomo won 82 percent of the vote.[53] Four years later, his successor Governor Kathy Hochul won only 70 percent of NYC.[54] While this preponderance of the majority of New York State was enough to secure reelection for Hochul, the huge realignment of New York City propelled challenger Congressman Lee Zeldin to a very tight overall race. Over four years, the Democrat/Republican vote in New York City moved a staggering 27 percent net.[55] Such swings in such a short period of time are rare.

---

[53] Steve Cortes, "Trump's Top 10 Achievements for 2019" (*Real Clear Politics*, December 31, 2019), https://www.realclearpolitics.com/articles/2019/12/31/trumps_top_10_achievements_for_2019_142047.html.

[54] Ibid.

[55] Matthew Thomas, "Can Democrats Survive the Looming Crisis in New York City's Outer Boroughs?" (Substack: Vulgar Marxism, January 25, 2023), https://vulgarmarxism.substack.com/p/can-democrats-survive-the-looming?utm_source=%2Fsearch%2Fvulgar%2520marxism&utm_medium=reader2.

So how and why did it happen?

Before getting into the positives for the movement and Republicans, let's establish that the improvement did not, at all, emanate from liberal, wealthy Manhattan. In fact, the credentialed elites of the Upper West Side and downtown Chelsea remained politically devoted to the Democrats, supporting Kathy Hochul enthusiastically despite her disastrous mismanagement of New York on a host of issues, from rampant crime to draconian COVID-19 measures. In fact, regarding the boroughs of New York City as counties, the most Democrat county in all of America rotated from the Bronx to Manhattan.[56]

Why this rotation?

The answer, primarily: Hispanics. Even as white leftists stayed dutifully in the Democrat tent, the brown patriots of New York City moved politically rightward. Zeldin shocked the political classes of Manhattan and Albany with his strong showing in the Bronx, one of the poorest and most diverse places in America.[57] In fact, the Bronx is only 9 percent white. But back in 2020, President Donald Trump showed real promise there, with a significant percentage surge in the Bronx during his four-year term. From 2016 to 2020, Trump doubled his raw vote total in the Bronx, and increased his percentage margin by 12 percent.[58] Then, in 2022, Lee Zeldin ran on a Trump-aligned platform of patriotic populism and won 22 percent of the vote. That total

---

56 Michael Lange, "The Fallout in New York" (Substack: The Narrative Wars, November 10, 2022), https://www.michaellange.nyc/p/the-fallout-in-new-york.

57 United States Census Bureau, "QuickFacts: Bronx County, New York" (U.S. Census Bureau) https://www.census.gov/quickfacts/fact/table/bronxcountynewyork/PST045221. Accessed June 13, 2024.

58 "2016 New York Presidential Election Results" (Politico, December 13, 2016), https://www.politico.com/2016-election/results/map/president/new-york/; "2020 New York Presidential Election Results" (Politico, January 6, 2021), https://www.politico.com/2020-election/results/new-york/.

might not seem impressive, but remember this was, until recent months, the most Democrat county in all America. Zeldin's performance improved another 12 percent net over the already-rallying 2020 results of Trump.[59]

The trend is clear. Working-class citizens move to the Right. Why? In large part because of populist economics; we live in an era of disenfranchisement for far too many regular laborers and their families, many of whom are Hispanics.

Continuing with the New York City analysis, the results in Queens reveal an even more promising trend for the movement. Queens is the most diverse county in the entire continental United States.[60] During the establishment, corporatist, Republican era, places such as Queens represented a political wasteland for conservatives. But now Queens should be viewed as a political octagon, a place to fight furiously to earn the support of a salt of the earth, diverse American population that has been abused by the ruling class and is ready to transfer its allegiance to a new political paradigm.

Consider, for example, in the majority Hispanic precincts of Queens, Zeldin earned almost triple the support Republicans got in 2018, from only 12 percent to 34 percent in 2022.[61] That math means, on margin, that the Democrats saw their Hispanic vote in Queens more than cut in half, from 76 percent in 2018 to 32 percent in 2022.

Some skeptics might try to claim that Hochul was just a bad candidate, even though she did win, or that Zeldin was a

---

59 "2016 New York Presidential Election Results."

60 Kaia Hubbard, "The 15 Most Diverse Counties in America" (U.S. News, August 24, 2021), https://www.usnews.com/news/health-news/slideshows/the-15-most-diverse-counties-in-the-us?slide=14.

61 Matthew Thomas, "Can Democrats Survive the Looming Crisis in New York City's Outer Boroughs?"

particularly good one. But the trend for years has been consistent and material in Queens—Hispanics continue to move away from Democrats.[62] Even if you take Hochul and Zeldin out of the equation, in 2014, Andrew Cuomo received 83 percent of the Hispanic vote in Queens. In 2016, Hilary Clinton got 85 percent. But then Biden declined to 76 percent in 2020, and Eric Adams to 67 percent in the 2021 mayoral race.

The trend is clear. It points to huge future gains for a GOP has that been transformed by the America First movement into a multi-ethnic, trans-racial party that represents a broad coalition of working-class citizens.

Americans of many colors and ethnicities recognize the intrinsic lack of economic opportunity they face. The ambitious strivers of Hispanic communities across America understand this harsh reality in a particular way, mainly because of the entrepreneurial bent of our familias.

In addition, they understand that these power structures created by the oligarchs suppress the ability of Hispanics to climb the economic ladder of success in America and participate in the abundance of this land the way previous immigrant groups did, such as the Irish and Italians. Wealth accumulation naturally propels assimilation and integration into the fullness of American life. The present barriers constructed by the ruling class act as a depressant to such upward mobility, and Hispanics smartly reject this paradigm.

So, the new paradigm, the new agenda must focus on the three key pillars of the patriotic populist movement: restoring sovereignty, resurrecting our culture, and promoting economic populism. In this third realm—the diffusion of economic

---

62 Ibid.

power—Hispanics quickly become the most vital national component of entrepreneurial renewal.

One such entrepreneur is Rick Figueroa of Texas. I met Rick when we were both honored with an appointment to the White House Hispanic Prosperity Initiative. His story is exceptional as a Horatio Alger tale of rising from challenging circumstances to a position of success and influence, but it is also not atypical of the overall upward trajectory of aspirational Latino go-getters in enterprise.

He grew up in Bay City, Texas as the youngest of eight children. Bay City is a working-class community between Houston and Corpus Christi near the Gulf Coast. Like much of the region, it is majority-Hispanic. With a single mom working at the hospital kitchen, Rick was raised in a household with very few luxuries but an abundance of love from his devoted madre.

Rick's mom insisted that, despite their modest circumstances, he live focused on the principles of life that matter most regardless of one's economic station in life. She instilled her simple but profound "7 Rules:"

1. Get out of bed early.
2. Get to work.
3. Don't expect anyone to help you.
4. Help others whenever you can.
5. Pray every single day to Jesus.
6. Find a good woman and marry her.
7. Raise godly children.
8. Honor God in everything you do.

As a boy and young man, Rick strived to follow these rules, and he mostly stayed true to the admonitions and encouragements of his Latina version of a "tiger mom." After he graduated public high school, he found steady employment working at the Exxon station. He could afford a decent car and lived at home where his mama cooked for him. He was basically content, and he did not know professional role models to steer his economic aims a bit higher.

But his mother saw his potential and prodded him to enroll in college. Though reticent, he realized the nearby community college had a lot of pretty girls, so he submitted and enrolled part-time in night classes.

Soon a spark was lit. Rick started to thrive at Wharton County Community College. Ever since he was a student, Rick likes to joke about attending Wharton...only his version is not the hallowed Ivy League Warton School of Business found at the University of Pennsylvania in Philadelphia.

In addition to pretty girls, Rick found intellectual challenge and motivation at that junior college. He also embraced academic competition, and the poor kid from Bay City grew determined to outperform his peers, including those who might have enjoyed more advantages growing up.

Soon, this bad hombre realized that a four-year university would accelerate his path and lead him to a work life that involved more than just physical labor. He worked part time and earned an accounting degree at Texas A&M, becoming a lifelong loyal Aggie.

Rick secured several impressive jobs in the accounting world, moving up the ladder at Arthur Andersen and becoming an auditor at the energy giant Halliburton. His Spanish fluency proved invaluable for his positions because they often involved international businesses throughout Latin America. The kid from Bay

City became a solidly successful white-collar professional with a wonderful wife and a promising future.

But, like so many young bad hombres, an entrepreneurial fire burned within him, and Rick took the significant risk of a major career shift. He left a cushy salary to join the world of wealth management as a financial advisor. Rick relays how the pressure was immense as he took a serious salary cut with a pregnant wife and no material savings to cushion any financial shock.

So, with his professional back against the wall, Rick scraped and rallied. Working at first for large Wall Street firms known as wire houses, Rick built up a solid portfolio of wealthy clients. Many of his clients were (and are) Hispanics who implicitly trusted their fellow hombre with their hard-earned assets. Many of these clients succeeded in the bare-knuckle business of trash hauling. In the 1980s, when corporate giants began to roll up these small firms and consolidate the disjointed industry into large national players, many of these bad hombre entrepreneurs walked away with bountiful buyout checks from firms like Waste Management.

These newly wealthy Hispanics turned to Rick for his skill and integrity in managing their affairs. He possessed a rare combination of traits to earn that trust. On the hard skills side, his quantitative accounting skills informed a data-driven approach to portfolio management. But even more importantly, he lived with a Christian character that won over hardscrabble entrepreneurs. Moreover, he intrinsically understood the travails of ascending from the barrios to the highest echelons of Houston business.

That grit compelled Rick to take another big professional leap of faith in middle age. After decades of building a successful book of business as part of the large Wall Street firm, he started a partnership to co-found his own wealth management firm. Such a move represented a significant risk for a successful wealth manager in his fifties who could have easily serviced his existing book at a large firm all the way into his own comfortable retirement.

But the flame of entrepreneurial zeal still glimmered. Like so many Hispanics, Rick yearned to truly be his own boss. The jefe. In addition, his firm lurched to the Left and inserted itself squarely into the culture wars on the side of the woke mob. For example, he was precluded from hosting a Bible study at the company, but the firm sent out notification that any employee could change genders at will. In a later chapter, I will detail how crucial the cultural issues are in moving Hispanics to the political Right. Rick is one such example.

So Rick took the leap and started his new firm. The clients enthusiastically followed him and his partners, and Rick now leads one of the largest Hispanic-owned wealth management firms in America. He endeavors to hire and mentor young Latinos who display the same drive that he developed as a young man, striving to live up to the expectations of his devoted mother.

Along with business success, Rick achieves prominence in politics as well, being active and influential in conservative causes. He serves on the national board of the National Rifle Association, safeguarding our sacred Second Amendment rights. As previously mentioned, he was appointed to a senior White House commission by President Trump—the Hispanic Prosperity Initiative. That board gained some unintended publicity after we posed with President Trump in the Rose Garden to receive our commissioning.

Bob Unanue, the head of Goya Foods, made some fairly standard CEO-style remarks, praising President Trump for his economic leadership and his particular assistance to the Latino business community in America. But suddenly in reaction, the Left howled that the CEO of Goya, a staple brand for Hispanic kitchens across America, had somehow betrayed the Latino community by complimenting Trump. Predictably, Congresswoman Alexandria Ocasio-Cortez (no relation to me, I assure you) got involved and called for a national boycott of the largest Hispanic-owned business in America.

Thankfully, and paradoxically, the outcry totally backfired. Hispanics—and a lot of gringos who had never even heard of Goya before—rushed to stores to buy Goya products and nearly emptied shelves nationwide. The new commissioners, Rick, and I all stood in solidarity with Unanue and Goya, of course, and the leftist outrage mob was defeated. But such tests will continue and likely accelerate given the massive gains the patriotic populist movement continues to rack up among Hispanic citizens.

American greatness was never achieved through statist, secularist radicals. That model has been tragically pursued all over Latin America for centuries with a string of predictable failures and crises. Those of us with Latin heritage do not seek, in any sense, to replicate the failures of Latin America here in the United States. My father did not leave Colombia to see America travel down a similar path of political violence, left-wing economics, and public sector corruption.

After experiencing the ill effects of Latin American economics, Hispanics rally to policies promoting the precepts of subsidiarity. This philosophy teaches that decision-making power should generally be diffused to the most local, small-scale principals. This political and economic construct finds its roots firmly in Catholic social teaching, and therefore naturally makes sense to millions of Catholic Hispanics in America. But no matter what denomination or faith, the principles of economic distributivism create the most vibrant and long-term prosperous society possible.

Hispanics stand uniquely positioned to lead the renaissance toward just such a society of justice and abundance. Hispanics will form the vanguard forefront of a revitalization of America's economic promise.

From humble day laborers to rising entrepreneurs like Rick Figueroa and magnates like Bob Unanue, Hispanics comprise a key economic pillar of American renewal. We will defeat the oligarchs and promote a diffusion of economic power. We Hispanics will be the fire that lights a path back to a republic based on sovereignty, traditional Western culture, and economic populism.

HISPANICS AND AMERICA FIRST ECONOMICS

Hispanics are going to lead the revitalization of small business and the return of productive capacity back to the United States, as well as sourcing manufacturing away from China and toward our friends in Latin America.

Let's begin this analysis with a discussion of mice and men.

More particularly, about the landmark "Mouse Utopia" study from 1968 and its key relevance for both America's modern culture and economy and for Hispanics as leaders of a new and better American economy.[63] That study still attracts significant interest over a half century later because of its dire warnings about human beings and the need for personal connectivity and lives of activity and purpose.

Biologist John Calhoun constructed a near-perfect habitat for mice—their utopia—as a large scale, years-long National Institute

[63] Maris Fessenden, "How 1960s Mouse Utopias Led to Grim Predictions for Future of Humanity" (*Smithsonian Magazine*, February 16, 2015), https://www.smithsonianmag.com/smart-news/how-mouse-utopias-1960s-led-grim-predictions-humans-180954423/.

for Health experiment. The Science History Institute describes the habitat:

> It was a large pen—a 4½-foot cube—with everything a mouse could ever desire: plenty of food and water; a perfect climate; reams of paper to make cozy nests; and 256 separate apartments, accessible via mesh tubes bolted to the walls. Calhoun also screened the mice to eliminate disease. Free from predators and other worries, a mouse could theoretically live to an extraordinarily old age there, without a single worry.[64]

As you might have already guessed, this supposed mice heaven quickly devolved into mice hell. At first, things went swimmingly for the furry little rodents. Calhoun put just eight mice in the structure to start, and the population doubled every couple of months, leading to a crowded twenty-two hundred mice in just a year and a half.

After that mice population apex, things turned south, and quickly. First, because there were no external threats, the male mice turned into either violent, unprovoked predators against each other, or they turned into self-absorbed pampered loners that only cared about grooming and looking good. The hierarchy that existed in the early days of the commune dissolved, and there were few rules or protections for mice families any longer. In fact, the female mice soon abandoned their own children, and birth rates fell. Within five years, the population of mice plunged from

64 Sam Kean, "Mouse Heaven or Mouse Hell?" (Science History Institute Museum and Library: *Distillations Magazine*, May 17, 2022), https://www.sciencehistory.org/stories/magazine/mouse-heaven-or-mouse-hell/.

2,200 to zero. Mouse heaven descended into rodent hell, and the mice were extinct.

Sound familiar?

Obviously, a study of mice does not definitively prove anything about the path of humans broadly or Americans specifically. However, this study still fascinates us decades later because many of us believe it contains relevant lessons for contemporary society. At the very least, the scientist leading the experiment believed it was all allegory and foreshadowed the potential future of humans.

Regarding the United States particularly, in many ways the success of the American way of life sowed the seeds for the potential destruction of that very prosperity. For centuries, the United States faced constant, fairly obvious threats and grand challenges. Until a century ago, taming the continent occupied much of the country's energy and vision. Manifest Destiny provided a framework ethos that compelled constant expansion led by brave pioneers who embodied the best of America. These pioneers, mostly men, were cheered on by all of society, even those who chose to remain in the relative safety of the east.

Once the American continent was subdued and firmly part of America, external threats rose and similarly occupied the mindset of the country and consumed much of the energy of the emerging power. America provided the decisive balance fighting in two successive world wars, and it grew into a power as dominant as any the world has ever known in the late 1940s and into the 1950s. Relative to the rest of the globe, America's grit, prestige, and raw power reigned over a world that was still badly broken from WWII.

But the giant new threat of communism grew, and the Cold War basically replaced the "hot wars" that preceded it. Through proxy battles across the world and incredible strength at home, America triumphed economically and socially in the grand struggle, sending Soviet-style Marxism to the ash heap of history.

But with the Cold War won and prosperity the norm at home, America found itself doddering and listless into the 1990s. Utopia-like pronouncements about a New World Order abounded and formed part of the naive, childish approach of the American establishment toward global trade and international interventionism.

We pursued reckless, international, so-called free trade while also initiating a series of major disastrous war interventions across the globe. These involvements, beginning with the wrongheaded first Gulf War under President George H. W. Bush, cost the United States dearly in American blood and treasure.

Even more damaging than the warmongering DC foreign policy establishment was Bill Clinton and George W. Bush's bipartisan agreement with the ruling class about unilaterally opening American markets to China in 2001. Beijing was allowed to enter the World Trade Organization on terms that were incredibly favorable to the Chinese regime.

Even though the Chinese Communist Party made no real concessions regarding its severe internal repression and slave labor practices, the garbage elites of America saw the potential for big personal profits at the expense of regular working-class Americans. The crux of the deal was this setup: Americans got a lot of cheap stuff from China to buy off the masses. In return, China would not open up to American exports of goods and services, but it would become America's factory instead as multinationals rushed to relocate thousands of plants and lay off millions of US workers in the process.

Some bargain for American citizens, huh?

Here is the point: Life had become easy, at least for the credentialed elites. There seemed to be no obvious external threat and certainly no grand countrywide challenge to pursue. The ruling class of America became soft and selfish, a lot like the mice in "Mouse Utopia." These leaders of politics and business slouched into the exact opposite of Teddy Roosevelt. They were squishy men consumed with manipulating a system for their personal benefit rather than dreamers daring to build great legacies.

The results for regular Americans were disastrous. A foreign invasion of America probably would have resulted in less damage to the homeland than the "free trade" agenda of the ruling class globalists. For one thing, there was no free trade, it was always managed, and it was structured to create maximum profits for the C suite officers of giant corporations, inflicting maximum pain upon America's manufacturing capacity and workers.

According to the Economic Policy Institute, America has lost a staggering 3.7 million jobs to China since Beijing's 2001 admission into the WTO.[65] Of those jobs, the vast majority were in manufacturing.[66] Those kinds of factory jobs are high-paying, family-sustaining positions, most of which do not require lofty credentials like an advanced degree. The ancillary fallout from this hallowing out of America's factories has been pervasive and pernicious. Entire communities lost hope, drug and alcohol addiction spiked, and pessimism spread like a disease.

---

[65] Robert E. Scott, "China Trade Deal Will Not Restore 3.7 Million U.S. Jobs Lost Since China Entered the WTO in 2001," January 13, 2020, epi.org/blog/china-trade-deal-will-not-restore-3-7-million-u-s-jobs-since-china-entered-the-wto-in-2001/.

[66] Robert E. Scott and Zane Mokhiber, "Growing China Trade Deficit Cost 3.7 Million American Jobs Between 2001 and 2018," January 30, 2020, epi.org/publication/growing-china-trade-deficits-costs-us-jobs/.

Combined with the 2008–2009 bailouts of Wall Street, this untenable situation for middle America led directly to the Tea Party movement, the most potent new political movement since the rise of the activist Left in the 1960s. In turn, the Tea Party organizations led directly to the 2016 America First movement, which then took national power with the upset victory of President Trump that November.

Since that time, this movement has successfully taken the Republican Party—at least at the voter level. Legacy office holders and donors have not fully subscribed to this new version of the GOP as a workers' party. In fact, the old guard of the party still dominates at the decision-making level in many ways, but all of the grassroots energy points to an inevitable, full takeover of the GOP as a populist nationalist party that prioritizes workers first.

These promising new trends flow from a counter-reaction against the abuses of globalism, which could have been predicted via mice, believe it or not!

Connecting these phenomena to Hispanics explains why so many Latinos rally to the political Right. A slight majority of the Hispanic community still considers themselves to be Democrats. But even those Latinos increasingly find themselves isolated and maligned by their own party. The Democratic Party of the 2020s is not your parents or grandparents' Democratic Party.

Gone are the figures like John F. Kennedy, Scoop Jackson, or Tip O'Neil. At the local level, there are no more Richard J. Daley's (the older Daley). Today's Democrats are committed Marxists who have entered into an unholy alliance with Big Business to pursue a globalist, secular humanist agenda that crushes the concept of the family and makes it nearly impossible to support a family on a single middle-class income.

Pro-family Hispanics reject this new, harsh economic reality!

As a matter of public policy, it is not the place of government to tell anyone they must stay home to care for children, look after elderly relatives, or fulfill other duties of the hearth. But it is very much the proper role of government to create the conditions that allow for a family to thrive on a single income.

This issue about single-income families matters to all middle and lower-income citizens, of course, and not just Hispanics. But since nearly all Latinos are statistically not wealthy (yet!), and since our communities still place such an intense importance on families, these issues resonate especially strongly with Hispanics.

When I grew up in the 1970s in a middle-class suburb on the south side of Chicago, nearly every household in my pleasant but modest neighborhood was supported by a single income with a caregiver at home—almost always women in those days. In fact, such an arrangement was the norm across American society for generations. It then suddenly went away in a seismic societal shift, and yet we hardly even talk about it, much less analyze the preferences of real people in this regard.

Many factors contributed to this shift, and some of them might even be considered positive. But the single most important contributing cause was globalization. That process began in the 1970s and then went into overdrive following China's entry into the World Trade Organization. A big part of the resulting economic carnage was a newfound necessity of two incomes to support a middle-class lifestyle in America. The current reality, truth be told, is that even two incomes cannot support a middle-class lifestyle under Joe Biden. But before Biden, most families could get by on dual-earners.

But should America return to an economic model that enables families to choose if more than one wage earner works outside of the home? Critics will assail my thinking as anachronistic and, of course, somehow sexist.

But the reality is that women themselves tell us they want to at least have the choice. If they leverage that opportunity into a career, then their decision is no one else's business. But providing the choice, the option, should very much be a foremost task of public policy.

Let's look at the data. Gallup Poll learned that the majority (56 percent) of women with children in the home prefer to be homemakers rather than work outside the home (39 percent).[67] Surprisingly, at least to me, even among women without children in the home, 39 percent of them preferred a homemaker role as opposed to working outside of the home.

In a related study with polling from American Compass, the results for working-class families were even more pronounced. Among these families, a stunning 71 percent prefer a traditional family structure, meaning they do not want both parents working full time.[68] These working-class families may not have fancy diplomas or credentials, but they seem to grasp well what author G.K. Chesterton observed over a century ago: "The most extraordinary thing in the world is an ordinary man and an ordinary woman and their ordinary children."

G.K. Chesterton also wrote extensively about the economic principles of subsidiarity, a concept that flows mainly from

---

67 Lydia Saad, "Children a Key Factor in Women's Desire to Work Outside the Home" (*Gallup News*, October 7, 2015), https://news.gallup.com/poll/186050/children-key-factor-women-desire-work-outside-home.aspx.

68 Steve Cortes, "Welcoming Back the Traditional, One-Income Family" (The National Pulse, July 2, 2021), https://thenationalpulse.com/archive-post/cortes-agenda-for-one-income-families/.

Catholic doctrine. Subsidiarity holds that economic power should be broadly diffused, and policy decisions should be based on how well economic power and rewards are dispersed across a society. To be clear, this approach is not socialist at all. Socialist, Marxist principles believe in dispersing resources by force to form a central command authority. Such models never work in practice, of course, and always lead to tyranny and violence.

But subsidiarity, properly understood, pursues policies to ensure a just and open country by spreading power and resources throughout society broadly. For example, G.K. Chesterton would be rightly appalled at the incredible concentration of economic power in America today. We have allowed the Left to create a winner-take-all system where oligopolies in industries like Big Money, Big Tech, and Big Pharma dominate massive swaths of American business and society. Moreover, the oligarchs who truly run American decision-making today—men like Jeff Bezos, Mark Zuckerberg, and Jamie Dimon—wield outsize power that dwarfs anything exercised by the so-called robber barons. For all his success and power, John D. Rockefeller is minimized by the power of the CEO of Google/Alphabet today, Sundar Pichai.

These problems are deeply entrenched, and these oligarchs will not willingly surrender power, of course. For example, Zuckerberg directly intervened in the 2020 election, giving hundreds of millions of dollars of his own money to practically ensure that Donald Trump would not win key swing states, especially Wisconsin and Pennsylvania. He pursued this election interference scheme via supposed "charitable funds," which made the unjust and illegal intrusion even worse. But it served as a blatantly public example of just how powerful these oligarchs are and just how seriously they guard their massive power.

But, like so many tough problems facing our country, Hispanics form the crux of the solution. This book's chapter on entrepreneurship discussed at length the start-up zeal of the Latino community in America. We are the heart and soul of a small business spirit that can lead a return to healthy, Main Street capitalism in America again—a small business spirit that would please G.K. Chesterton.

Starting a new venture requires guts and determination. It requires a willingness to toil seemingly endless hours, particularly in the early days of any enterprise. Hispanics display these attributes on steroids, as evidenced by the outlier statistics on business formation in the Hispanic community.

Since I have focused considerably on the leadership role of Hispanic men in forging America's renewal, this topic provides an opportune time to also praise the impressive gains of proud Latina women. While Hispanics overall continue to massively outperform in the category of start-ups, 40 percent of those new operations are headed by Latina women.[69] Those Latina entrepreneurs now own over two million small businesses that have enjoyed a stunning growth rate of 87 percent since 2007, according to the National Women's Business Council.[70]

That kind of success, proven by those kinds of statistics, points to a better future where Hispanic entrepreneurs lead the way, serving as economic trailblazers toward a better economy with more rewards for regular workers and less concentration of wealth and power among the managerial elites.

---

69 Elizabeth Rios, "Latina Business Owners Making a Difference in the Community" (*Latin Business Today*), https://latinbusinesstoday.com/latina-business-owners-making-a-difference-in-the-community/. Accessed June 13, 2024.

70 Ibid.

That discussion of revitalizing Main Street via small business naturally leads back to a macro analysis of trade, looking to find the ways in which policy can reform corrupted practices in pursuit of a far more prosperous American middle class, including Hispanics. This policy reform must begin with tariffs and other protective measures.

Of course, even the term "protectionism" rankles most power brokers on the Right. We are supposedly a movement dedicated to free trade. Of course, as detailed throughout this book, there has never been free trade, especially not after the World Trade Organization welcomed the Chinese Communist Party with open arms. That welcome team, incidentally, included a wide array of bipartisan business executives and politicians, including Bill Clinton, Al Gore, George W. Bush, Barack Obama, and Joe Biden.

For decades prior to the 2016 election, Republican and conservative orthodoxy held that free trade must be pursued as an ipso facto goal—a good in and of itself. They thought comparative advantage compelled goods and services to be sourced wherever they could most cheaply be produced, without consideration of other factors. America plunged headfirst into this agenda with little concern of the fallout for US workers and a naive expectation that other countries would match our openness and respond with reciprocal and fair access to their domestic markets.

Of course, the opposite trend unfolded, and China was the single most abusive culprit. American companies who were allowed into China to try to sell to its domestic market were met with constant hurdles and harassment. Some of these obstacles were overt, outright prohibitions. But often the frustrations were subtler, involving powerful CCP bureaucrats using the vast levers of the state apparatuses within China to make life difficult for US firms. This was especially pertinent for smaller companies trying to gain a foothold in the Middle Kingdom. The *Wall Street Journal* recently reported on this macro trend with a story headlined "American Business Stalls in China."[71]

In addition, even for those companies that were able to operate successfully in China, getting capital and profits out of the country proved nearly impossible. Meanwhile, we opened American commercial gates wide for Chinese products, welcoming everything from cheap junk like plastic toys to key products like pharmaceuticals and semiconductors.

China is the worst and most important trade abuser of America by any measure. But Beijing is hardly alone in using one-sided, predatory trade practices against the United States. For example, South Korea has developed into an incredible growth story for decades, basically since the end of the Korean War. After America fought to keep Seoul free from the communist North, we opened our markets to South Korean products. This openness probably made sense from a geostrategic perspective.

After all, holding South Korea was a key win for America in the Cold War, though it cost thousands of American lives and great financial sacrifice from US taxpayers. But Korea, to its credit, largely modeled the United States' approach to trade during the early years of the American republic, and it still does. Korea protects domestic businesses while taking full advantage of access to US markets.

---

[71] Newley Purnell and Clarence Leong, "American Business Stalls in China" (*Wall Street Journal: Business,* March 27, 2024), https://www.wsj.com/business/american-companies-china-trade-exports-eb49310d

For example, the average tariff that Korea places on imported agricultural goods from America is a whopping 54 percent.[72] In comparison, the average equivalent tariff for goods inbound to America is 9 percent. Outside of agriculture, Korean tariffs overall are more than twice as high as America's—and yet Korea enjoys tremendous growth and prosperity. All the while, by the way, America continues to defend Korea with a massive troop presence. So we station tens of thousands of Americans abroad to defend the Korean peninsula, and in turn, the nation pursues a very rational economic agenda of protection for Korean industry—one that prioritizes Korean jobs while taking full advantage of America's dogmatic commitment to alleged free trade. Sound like a good deal for the United States?

As referenced earlier, it was not always this way for our country. The system from the early American republic helped our nation transform from an agrarian society into an industrial powerhouse. This economic agenda was pioneered by Alexander Hamilton, who was probably the most gifted political leader overall in American history. The plan involved a stable currency and protection for American industry. This philosophy found important political torchbearers after the days of the Founding Fathers, first via Henry Clay, and then through Abraham Lincoln. The sixteenth president was an ardent believer in protectionism, declaring that he was "in favor of a high protective tariff."[73] Lincoln also warned a joint session of Congress that any "abandonment of

---

72 "Learn Key Facts About the U.S.-South Korea Trade Agreement" (Office of the United States Trade Representative), https://ustr.gov/uskoreaFTA/key_facts. Accessed June 13, 2024.

73 "Washington and Lincoln Were Tariff Men" (*Wall Street Journal: Opinion*, December 12, 2018), https://www.wsj.com/articles/washington-and-lincoln-were-tariff-men-11544632083.

the protective policy by the American government [will] produce want and ruin among our people."[74]

What prophetic words indeed from the man who saved the American union. If only Honest Abe could have addressed Congress before we bowed down to the CCP and ushered Beijing right into America via trade! But Lincoln was hardly alone among Republican luminaries who endorsed the efficacy of protecting American workers and industries. President William McKinley opined that "the foreign producer has no right or claim to equality with our own…He contributes nothing to the support, the progress, and the glory of the Nation."[75] His successor Teddy Roosevelt remarked, "Thank God I am not a free trader." Looking outside of partisan politics, the US Constitution itself prescribes import duties to "regulate Commerce with foreign Nations," and it makes no reference whatsoever to so-called free trade.

Realize, as well, that this protection is necessary not because Americans are unable to compete with foreign firms on a fair, level playing field. Instead, they are necessary because nearly all the nations of the world aggressively manage trade in their own interests, often with massive explicit or implicit subsidies of their own businesses. How can a US firm, therefore, compete against a Chinese steel producer backed by the CCP that is unconcerned with real, auditable profits? The answer is that it cannot succeed, nor should it be compelled to even try!

Repairing and rebuilding the industrial might of America by restoring domestic production will broadly assist society, especially the lives of working-class citizens. But Hispanics will benefit

---

74 Daniel Pearson, "Lincoln was wrong on trade" (The Hill, March 1, 2017), https://thehill.com/blogs/pundits-blog/economy-budget/321843-lincoln-was-wrong-on-trade/.

75 "Washington and Lincoln Were Tariff Men."

disproportionately, and this should be embraced as an aspect of smarter trade policy. For instance, Latinos are so dominant in the building trades that a mass movement to refurbish or construct new production facilities in the United States would be a bonanza for Hispanic America.

A new "American System" economic model would also benefit Hispanics through another production goal—bringing operations to nearby countries. Our first priority should be returning industries here to the United States. In fact, for key national security industries like medicines and computer chips, it must be compelled, not just encouraged.

But we do also recognize that America First never meant America Alone. Protecting American industry as a priority does not mean that international trade ceases. Instead, a new "American System" would require that trade be reciprocal and fair, forming a true two-way partnership where significant comparative advantages can make each country better off as a result of the intercountry commerce.

For example, we do not grow coffee in the United States. Most American adults begin every day with java—I know I certainly do. We obviously need foreign products. Coffee-blessed nations like Colombia and Brazil love American movies, and no one dominates the pop culture businesses like the creative class of the United States. So we send movies to them, and they send coffee to us. A simple but profound example, and everyone wins. But let me give a negative example. Both America and Brazil are massive soybean producers. We have different growing seasons, which helps facilitate trade between the countries during offseasons. But if the leftist government of Brazil decided to subsidize beans and undercut American producers, we should absolutely use trade barriers and tariffs to protect American agriculture.

That hypothetical aside, we maintain mostly warm and beneficial trade relationships with Latin America, especially with our neighbor Mexico. In this regard, when we do trade internationally, instead of allowing China to economically pillage America, why not give preference to our friendly allies south of our border?

This process has already begun, in large part thanks to Trump's tariffs upon China. For the first time in years, total trade with Mexico now exceeds total trade with China.[76] After two decades of China as the leading importer into the United States, Mexico now takes the number one position for imported goods into America. It is hard to overstate the importance of this trend and the urgency to accelerate it going forward.

So we have an existing trend that just needs some nurturing to become a much bigger economic force. A burgeoning trade with Mexico and the rest of Latin America would concurrently serve myriad US interests. First, it reduces our reliance on China and the overall power of the Chinese Communist Party. The CCP presents an existential threat to America, and we should never trade with our sworn enemies. We did not trade with the USSR nor with Imperial Japan. We have not traded with communist Cuba since Castro took power, and that isolation is part of what has hobbled that regime for decades.

America's dependence on China was starkly exposed during the COVID-19 panic and lockdowns. The inability to get goods from China caused massive disruptions to US life and commerce,

[76] Paul Wiseman, "Mexico overtakes China as the leading source of goods imported by US" (AP News, February 7, 2024), https://apnews.com/article/china-goods-imports-trade-mexico-tariffs-trump-eaee6cec8bb3cadc1103ba60f986b76e.

and it opened many eyes about just how intertwined the US economy had become with Beijing.

Greater trade with Latin America would also build prosperity in our southern neighbors, creating domestic environments that are less likely to send masses of migrants to America's door seeking illegal entry. A more prosperous Latin America, not a wealthier CCP, best serves American interests.

In addition, building goodwill within the greater Americas represents a sound strategy for America's long-term global standing, one sure to please millions of Hispanic American citizens who pledge allegiance to Old Glory but still naturally hold affinity for their ancestral homelands and want the best for Latin America.

Latin leftists have long accused America of pseudo-colonialism in our approach to the rest of the Americas. Though exaggerated, those accusations to flow from partial truth. Outside of the Spanish-American War, we never sought colonies in Latin America, but we have often treated our "neighborhood" with benign neglect. Through much of US history, we have mostly ignored our southern neighbors, while occasionally punctuating that indifference with interventions that locals legitimately view as heavy-handed.

But the past is spilled milk and cannot be changed in the here and now. What *can* change is US economic policy and our overall approach to Latin America. Again, the first priority of American economic renewal must be the relocation of production back to the United States itself. This process will hugely benefit bad hombres and proud Latinas. This process will also assist in reinvigorating our own country's small businesses, as they will become suppliers to the plants that will be built and operate within our borders.

When America does look outside its border for commercial reasons, the first priority should be Latin America, and the last priority should be China. Of course, shifting course in such a macro sense is not easy, nor is it quick. Because of the failings of the US ruling class, our country is still very dependent upon China for the American way of life to even function.

But, with dedication of purpose and laser focus, in the coming years we can wean off the unhealthy reliance upon our enemy, the CCP. We can, and must, replace the most critical processes of production back to the United States, but we should use Latin America, and Mexico especially, as our preferred partner when we engage in intercountry exchanges.

Regarding movement across the border, the free flow of goods across the US-Mexico demarcation can only improve if the United States determines to regain control of the American side of the border. Joe Biden, Kamala Harris, and Alejandro Mayorkas did not just tolerate mass illegality at the border, but in fact incentivized and welcomed this tragic human tsunami of trespassers who have essentially vaporized the US border. The Biden administration abdicated its first duty—to secure public order.

This lawlessness also created an unsurpassed opportunity for Mexican cartels to establish an order—albeit a criminal one—over that side of the border line. Right now, the Mexican side is completely controlled by the Mexican cartels. The cartels love this arrangement for two reasons. First, smuggling people is even more profitable for those Mexican mafias than smuggling narcotics. Second, the unending flow of unvetted migrants into America creates nonstop opportunities to transport drugs and other contraband into America.

This created border crisis results in perhaps the largest transfer of wealth to a criminal network in all history. The US House Budget Committee, for example, estimates that an additional $1 billion per month flows into the cartels for human smuggling as a result of the invited Biden border chaos.[77] This influx of cold cash makes the already powerful cartels effectively a quasi-state actor within Mexico. This development makes it more difficult for the Mexican military and law enforcement to curtail the power of the cartels.

So, before any further progress can unfold regarding trade with Mexico, the border must be secured. Once we establish an orderly flow of legal goods and people, the process of relocating trade with Latin America can and should accelerate.

That flow should extend throughout the Americas, of course. For example, having strong new leaders makes eminent sense for all countries involved. The recent work of President Nayib Bukele in El Salvador, for example, has been amazing; he quickly turned one of the world's most dangerous nations into a place of calm and order in just a few years. In 2023, the homicide rate of El Salvador plunged by 70 percent, making it the country with the second lowest murder rate in the Americas after Canada.[78] This kind of tranquility in a country that was overrun with gang violence for decades represents a remarkable achievement.

No wonder Bukele is so popular and overwhelmingly won reelection. His support among American Latinos grows as well,

---

[77] Jessica M. Vaughan, "Biden Border Policies Are Working Fine—For the Cartels" (Center for Immigration Studies, February 5, 2024), https://cis.org/Vaughan/Biden-Border-Policies-Are-Working-Fine-Cartels.

[78] Nelson Renteria, Valentine Hilaire, and Rosalba O'Brien, "El Salvador says murders fell 70% in 2023 as it cracked down on gangs" (Reuters, January 3, 2024), https://www.reuters.com/world/americas/el-salvador-says-murders-fell-70-2023-it-cracked-down-gangs-2024-01-03/.

as Hispanic citizens long for some of the same tough on crime, law-and-order tactics to restore peace to US cities.

Looking back at the US domestic scene, there are millions of Bukele figures among the tens of millions of Hispanics in the United States. The vast majority of these Hispanics in America will not rise to such political prominence as Bukele himself, of course. But they can, and will, serve as similarly remarkable and determined leaders in their own communities, churches, and businesses. In contrast to the soft and self-indulgent "Mouse Utopia" potentates of the ruling class, this emerging leadership cohort of bad hombres and proud Latinas will forge a path of renewal for America, particularly economically. With smarter policies regarding small business, trade, and the border, these Hispanics will become the lifeblood of a restored and more prosperous America that is reclaimed from the oligarchs.

MEDIA AND HISPANICS

As Hispanics across America dive more deeply into politics, they confront a media landscape that is largely hostile to their values and traditions. Historically, Hispanics have simply not been as politically engaged as other demographics, especially compared to the black community in America. In some ways this aversion to politics was a benefit; it allowed Latinos to focus on work, family, and self-created success instead of succumbing to politicized narratives and the constant quest for political favor.

But, like so many Americans who were formerly apolitical or at least not highly politically engaged, the hands of Hispanics have been forced by the Left. You see, the modern Democratic Party has no intention of simply leaving bad hombres and proud Latinas alone. For starters, Democrats refuse to acknowledge objective reality, and they will not even recognize the inherent differences and complementarity between those two sexes!

But even worse than general gender confusion, the Left insists on indoctrinating young children with toxic and unhealthy propaganda about sexuality through pop culture, school curricula, and draconian laws in places like California where parents can lose their rights over a child who suddenly suspects they were born the "wrong" sex.

Like all decent, God-fearing, children-loving Americans, Hispanics overwhelmingly reject this kind of radicalism. Consequently, Hispanics must enter the political arena with growing fervor to flex the considerable political muscle our communities can muster. But that process requires information. Activists and voters can only be effective when they are armed with the information necessary to truly move the needle on politics and culture.

Unfortunately, this process of learning issues and acquiring political process knowledge is largely perverted and corrupted by highly biased, dishonest gatekeepers—the media. In this regard, Hispanics have struggled to learn the truths about key issues, and they have often been misled when they mistakenly relied upon supposedly respectable platforms, ones that may have once served the public interest but now only function as public relations arms for the ruling class. This problem is prolific on the English-speaking media platforms, of course. But the media credibility crisis is even worse in Spanish-speaking media, as Univision and Telemundo, for example, often make MSNBC and ABC News seem fair and objective by comparison!

The Spanish-speaking media landscape recently got even worse with the large-scale purchase of Latino-focused radio properties by George Soros.[79] The leftist billionaire teamed up with Hollywood celebrities to purchase eighteen Spanish-language

[79] Allsides Technologies, Inc., "As Billionaire George Soros Takes Control of 235 Radio Stations, AllSides Offers Path to Protect Media Integrity" (PR Newswire, February 20, 2024), https://www.prnewswire.com/news-releases/as-billionaire-george-soros-takes-control-of-235-radio-stations-allsides-offers-path-to-protect-media-integrity-302066490.html.

stations in the largest cities in America, including the flagship Cuban-focused station Radio Mambi in Miami, Florida.[80]

That Miami station had always served as a strong media voice against the Left. Its audience was mostly comprised of the Cuban diaspora community of South Florida who migrated to the United States on a large scale to escape the tyranny of dictator Fidel Castro in Havana. So, with this takeover from the most radical, Marxist elements of the American Left, expect the propaganda efforts of Spanish-dominant media to worsen, at least in the near term.

But even aside from the highly biased Spanish-language organizations, the approach to Latinos and Latino issues in the regular English-dominant media properties has been problematic for years. A successful, long-term upsurge for the Hispanic Right will require new and better media companies to inform and arm Latino patriots.

I have some expertise on these issues as I have been on daily TV, mostly national cable news programming, for most of the last seventeen years. My own experiences in TV news, both on camera and behind-the-scenes, have shaped my views about general media corruption and how it relates to Hispanics more specifically.

For example, I might be the only person in media today who has been a paid commentator on all three of the largest cable news channels. I started my TV career at the NBC Universal network, mostly doing CNBC and some MSNBC programs. I then worked for Fox News/Fox Business before working for CNN.

---

80 Dana Kennedy, "Radio stars criticize George Soros-backed move to 'silence conservative Hispanic voices'" (*New York Post*, December 20, 2022), https://nypost.com/2022/12/20/inside-george-soros-backed-move-to-silence-conservative-hispanic-voices/.

In addition, I served as a principal spokesman for the 2016 and 2020 Trump campaigns and as national spokesman for Ron DeSantis in 2023. Outside of presidential politics, I also served as a spokesman for some key Senate candidates and their victorious races, especially J.D. Vance of Ohio and Katie Britt of Alabama. I have done hundreds and hundreds of live TV interviews, from largely attended national broadcasts down to small market local news shows.

In addition to my TV work, I have also become a prolific writer, getting hundreds of political opinion pieces published in the *Wall Street Journal*, *Newsweek*, *Pittsburgh Post-Gazette*, *Milwaukee Journal Sentinel*, and *Real Clear Politics*, just to name a few.

I also hosted an afternoon drive-time radio show in Chicago from 2020 to 2021 in the third biggest market in America. The *Steve Cortes Show* on WIND station was a great opportunity for me, but I ultimately learned that I much prefer the medium of TV over radio for best utilizing my talents as a communicator.

So, given this deep well of media experience on both the broadcast and print sides, I have learned a lot about the broken business model of most of the current media, the inherent contradictions and conflicts of interest that characterize all the legacy platforms, and the harm done to our republic by a discredited press. In addition, I have learned about the particular harm done to Hispanic citizens, as they have grown into more politicized roles in our society out of necessity.

My beginnings in media grew out of my Wall Street job as a bond trader and broker. My good friend Dennis Gartman recommended me for CNBC, and that simple request from a friend changed my professional life. Gartman was the author and editor of the *Gartman Letter*, which was a sort of morning paper for the capital markets community around the world. Starting with a letter he faxed out to a small group of subscribers in the 1980s, Dennis grew his morning missives into a small empire widely read by thousands around the world who paid close attention to his strategic views on markets and politics.

Because I put out similar notes to high-end institutional traders in the United States and Europe, Dennis and I crossed paths and became good friends.

His business really took off when he became a regular commentator on CNBC. Once he was established there and employed as a contributor—meaning the network paid him for exclusivity to that channel—he recommended me for some TV tryouts.

When CNBC first called, I literally thought it was a prank. But it was real. I was in New York at the time on business travel, and they sent a black car to pick me up for meetings at their headquarters and studios just across the Hudson River in Englewood Cliffs, New Jersey.

I assumed I was merely going for some discussions about possibly being on-air, but within about fifteen minutes of talking shop with the legendary producer there, Susan Krakower, she put me right on TV. I appeared again that night on *Fast Money*, the 5 p.m. EST show that broadcasts from the Nasdaq MarketSite in Times Square.

It was quite the baptism by fire for someone who had never done one bit of media before. I appeared on two national broadcasts on my first day with zero training, preparation, or even guidance as to how I should handle live TV. Luckily, it came quite naturally to me…not that I wasn't nervous! In fact, for the first few months of television, I was incredibly nervous each time I appeared. In hindsight, I did a great job of hiding that trepidation from the audience and a decent job of concealing it from other folks on the sets of CNBC, but it was palpable internal fear for the first few months. However, after enough reps, like anything in life, it became second nature, and the nervousness all went away.

On that theme though, even though I am now totally comfortable in any media setting and in front of any crowd, whether live or over the airwaves, I am careful to not allow myself to get complacent. Being comfortable on-air is a good thing, but slouching into cockiness or self-approbation would be terrible for the causes I work so hard to advance. When I coach other talent about how to be most effective on-air, I always recommend they follow my practice of watching tape. Just like a serious athlete, a communicator must watch themselves—and others who have great skill. I am my own toughest critic, and I cannot stand it when I see clips of myself saying something in a confusing manner or using "um" in on-air appearances.

For those of us on the Right, such self-reflection and tough self-criticism is especially important. Why? Because those of us who venture into the lions' dens of the mainstream media need to recognize that every show, each anchor, and all the producers are simply dying for a moment when they can embarrass you or make you look dumb. That harsh reality reveals the bias and corruption of the corporate media, but it is simply the truth of the broad media landscape. As a consequence, to advance right-wing ideas on-air, the communicator better be twice as prepared and twice as talented.

But in my early days with CNBC back in 2008, I was hired to talk markets and stock tickers, not politics and policy. I joined the network just before the horrible Great Financial Crisis/Housing

Bust of 2008 and 2009. I also joined before Barack Obama was elected and took office, and my role there basically remained unconnected to his presidential race. I stuck to markets, and the channel mostly did, as well.

I cared a lot about politics personally. Like most concerned, patriotic Americans, I saw huge dangers in electing Obama—a fellow Chicagoan that even most Windy City residents had not even heard about just a few years prior. But as a market analyst, trader, and someone newly entrenched in business media, I also knew that the financial crisis of fall 2008 was so sweeping and frightening to Americans that they would almost surely opt for the promised "hope and change" of this charismatic young politician.

There was also a great hope that America's election of its first black president would be momentous for our country and further our incredible strides toward racial comity and healing. To this day, I concede that Obama's election was a major milestone for him personally and the country broadly. We elected a black man as commander-in-chief a century and a half after abolition, and that progress represents real, tangible achievement.

But unfortunately, Obama could not rise above himself and seize the incredible opportunity he had to become an agent of racial harmony in America. Instead, he headed in the opposite direction and actually did his best to gin up racial strife where it had not existed. He used every possible political occasion to call America racist and reignite racial tension that had been pushed aside prior to him taking office. Paradoxically, America's first black president used his power to foment new racism in both directions—black versus white.

This tragic outcome also points to why Hispanics, and Hispanics alone, can save this country. Whites have been relegated to a strange second-class status, and people of power always assume them to be guilty of some unspoken prejudice. Most ruling class whites themselves buy into this toxic self-loathing; they think white people today should be judged by the actions of people who happened to have white skin three, four, or ten generations ago.

Similarly, Obama convinced black Americans to fixate on their race as well, encouraging a victimhood mentality that belied the facts on the ground in twenty-first century America. Obama became the first member of a black leadership class that works for its own selfish gains by exploiting the masses of hardworking black citizens, seeking only political preferences and favors rather than strong black families and authentic, grassroots black prosperity.

So, who is the large group in America undeterred by either of these macro forces that were unleashed by Obama? It's Hispanics. Now, when I joined CNBC, I was not there to be a Latino broadcaster. I did not necessarily speak as a Hispanic or focus on Hispanic issues. Sure, the channel used me in some promos to prove they were "diverse," but I was simply a financial expert and an American, not a Hispanic.

But as a proud American and quiet right-winger, I saw the channel change measurably once Obama took office to really institute his agenda. In the fallout of the Housing Crisis, it was impossible to discuss markets without commenting on policy, since the federal government had become so active and controlling over huge swaths of the American economy.

Inevitably, when those discussions unfolded on-air, I was tough on Obama and pointed out policy errors, even though I did not at that time use the language of a political partisan or activist. But then the network started to morph into a platform that was stridently protective of Obama. This stand seemed especially strange to me at first, given that CNBC had operated very independently of the NBC and MSNBC ways in its pre-Obama days. In fact, as a business channel, CNBC tried to exalt the virtues of capitalism to a mostly center-right, male businessman audience.

But the network started to censor my comments on Obama, getting into my ear during live broadcasts and putting me into TV versions of "timeouts" where I was not booked for a string of days or weeks. Given that I was paid per appearance, such timeouts were effectively financial punishments as well.

I was soon told by a friendly producer on the sly that the orders were coming down from the corporate parent, General Electric, to lay off Obama. Then it all made sense to me. GE had effectively become a de facto department of the Obama administration. That conglomerate was enmeshed in every aspect of Obama's tenure, from Obamacare and defense contracting to government supports for GE Capital in the wake of the Housing Crisis fallout.

After all, it was under Obama and Biden that the fusion of big business and the permanent political class really took shape. Large multinational corporations had been creeping to the Left for decades, and they had long been getting more political and more aligned with the Democratic Party.

Since China had mistakenly been invited into the World Trade Organization, American trade with China exploded, though the United States faced far more repercussions as our trade deficit with Beijing went to the sky. Big business was all-in on sending American production to China, as they could exploit cheap labor there and then send those products back into America. In some cases, the labor was not just cheap, but it was actually free because the workers were actual or quasi-slaves serving the tyrannical masters of the Chinese Communist Party.

These corporate behemoths that so fully supported this hallowing out of America's productive capacity also largely controlled media assets in America to propagandize for this globalism. In the case of GE and NBC Universal, they utilized direct control. For many other companies like big banks and Big Pharma, their control has been more indirect—covering advertising, sponsorships, or programming.

Given these realities, it became obvious to me that I could not remain permanently at CNBC. I grew more political and more outraged at what Obama and Biden were doing to America, on both the economic and racial fronts. My TV employer, concurrently, was moving ever more into lockstep with the Democrats and big business. So the situation became untenable. In addition, after the Great Recession, the network just did not have the same juice it did before, through no fault of its own. The days of dentists and housewives all-day trading were simply over. Far too many people got burned, either in the dot-com bubble or in the credit crisis bubble, and some in both. The days of CNBC on every TV in every pub and gym in America were over. For a time, being a CNBC "trader" on-air had great benefits, and it certainly helped my Wall Street career immensely for a period, but that status changed over time.

But luckily for me, Fox News had started up Fox Business to compete with CNBC, and they hired away some of the best talent from Englewood Cliffs. I was quite close with two in particular, Trish Regan and Maria Bartiromo. They contributed to my move over to Fox News. I felt a bit of trepidation about leaving CNBC, but it was time. That network taught me so much about TV and communicating. There were, and are, some terrific people there. But as the channel changed, it was time for Steve Cortes' next media chapter.

The initial plan was for me to continue primarily as a business commentator and market analyst, talking currencies, interest rates, and tickers. But then an orange guy came down the escalator on Fifth Avenue and changed everything—for me and for America.

Trump won me over with his blunt and even brash take on populist nationalist economics. I wrote a book in 2011, *Against the Herd*, published by Wiley Publishing, a business books specialist.[81] The book's primary thesis argued against corporate America's obsession with China. I warned that investing there was foolish, the whole so-called emerging markets theme was far too exaggerated, and investing in America provided far better risk-adjusted returns for investors. I was also very brutal in detailing the abuses of the Beijing regime, calling them an international mafia and comparing them to the Corleone family in tactics.

Those descriptions may seem mainstream now, but they were way out in left field back in 2011. Wall Street was infatuated with China, and ruling class Americans simply ignored the abuses and dangers of the CCP as they found the new wave of investment and offshore production to be very personally profitable. The publisher warned me, for this reason, that an anti-China book going "against the herd" might not sell well—everyone wanted to believe China was the next economic frontier of opportunity.

They were partly right; it did not sell as much as I hoped, but it did well enough to make money, as CNBC generously allowed

---

81 Steve Cortes, *Against the Herd: 6 Contrarian Investment Strategies You Should Follow* (Wiley Books: December 13, 2011).

me to push it a lot on the channel. In fact, my anti-China thesis did create for some solid, contentious TV debates with other traders on the network who all loved the China story. Those showdowns, though basically friendly disagreements, set the stage for far more brutal TV battles I would have later once I fully joined Team Trump.

When Trump fully started to campaign against China on pro-economic protectionist themes, I fully converted, economically speaking. I left the squishy, comfortable ways of Wall Street republicanism and dove headfirst into the arena of populist nationalism.

Trump had the guts and smarts to talk about trade and China in ways that reinforced what I knew about China from an investing standpoint, and he opened my eyes to the dangers of America tolerating decades of porous border policies. Once I started speaking forcefully in favor of Trump and his campaign themes on-air, I became much more in demand on Fox News and Fox Business to discuss politics rather than just financial markets. Trump started to dominate media news cycles all over the dials of TV and radio, and soon I ceased talking markets at all and simply advocated for Trump.

People took notice at Trump Tower, including the candidate himself, who invited me to join his team. It was a still a total startup operation at that point in early 2016—very seat-of-the-pants. It was exciting and full of talented patriots but also chaotic and a bit rudderless. Still, I plunged into the effort and was soon positioned as the go-to guest for the toughest interviews. I volunteered my time and loved every minute of it, figuring that Trump probably could not win, but that we were moving the needle with public opinion. I guessed my foray into politics would be this wild but short ride and that I would return to "regular" TV and to my Wall Street career.

Wow, was I wrong!

Also, because I am Hispanic, I became a powerful voice against the scurrilous slander that Trump's strong border policies flow from some anti-Latino prejudice. As the son of an immigrant, I made the case that Hispanics are not soft on the border and that border lawlessness is most offensive to the millions of legal immigrants, like my own dad, who came to America the right, respectful way.

I also pointed out almost daily on TV that the dangerous people crossing the border with ill intent overwhelmingly inflicted their abuses upon Hispanic American citizens. In addition, the economic harm brought on by hordes of illegal workers fell disproportionately upon Hispanics working in the trades and other blue-collar fields that saw a huge influx of illegal alien workers.

Believe me, if illegal immigrants took the jobs of law partners, investment bankers, and media anchors, then the border would be hermetically sealed in about two seconds! No exaggeration. But since the working class suffers the consequences, the ruling-class people of influence simply do not care. Even worse, they often benefit because they love the cheap labor that makes their lives easier—the housekeepers, landscapers, and nannies that undercut the wages of American workers and boost the wealthiest in society.

In this regard, my ethnicity and father's story became a massive problem for the corrupt media. They had convinced themselves that Trump hates brown people overall and especially immigrants. Of course, that lazy calumny falls apart with any honest reporting, but it became the corporate media's default position. I was there to provide a face and voice to make the counter case. I also did so with a degree of broadcasting skill and smile, making the dishonest media charlatans even more enraged.

The media's approach unfortunately worked with some large segments of the Hispanic community in 2016, but it sure did not work by 2020, and it will not work at all into the 2024 election. Trump's performance in office won over so many hearts and minds of Latinos that the media narrative carries little power today, at least compared to 2016.

As an example, a 2024 Axios Harris poll asked Americans about Trump's mass deportation plans for a second term, and a majority of 51 percent support these policies.[82] I wish that number would head even higher, but it still shows just how much Americans revile the open-border lawlessness of Biden; they are willing to approve of a large-scale law enforcement effort that has not been attempted since the Eisenhower administration.

Contradicting media narratives, 45 percent of Hispanics in this poll also support mass deportations. It is not quite a majority, but a substantial minority of Hispanics support mass deportations, most of whom surely know someone who would get expelled. That 45 percent represents a groundswell shift. It is "yuge," as Trump would say. But note how Axios frames the story: "Americans are open to Trump's harshest immigration plans."[83] Axios also explains away the majority support as a consequence of "a relentless messaging war waged by Republicans."[84]

---

82 Margaret Talev and Russell Contreras, "Exclusive poll: America warms to mass deportations" (Axios, April 25, 2024), https://www.axios.com/2024/04/25/trump-biden-americans-illegal-immigration-poll.

83 Ibid.

84 Ibid.

Well, Axios, if there is a war being waged, it is by Biden. He throws open America's front door to welcome in unvetted masses of illegals, who compete in both the job market and the housing market against American citizens. And some members of this human tsunami of trespassers come with ill intent, looking to do harm to American citizens in totally preventable crimes that are enabled by open-border radicalism.

Also note that 42 percent of Democrat voters say they support Trump's large-scale deportation agenda, which perhaps highlights the growing disconnect between media organizations and their left-wing party. That is one number which surely scares the bejesus out of sharp Democrat campaign operatives.

That polling did get coverage from Fox News and right-wing accounts on social media, but it has been totally ignored by traditional media outlets. Why? It is simply too destructive to the "Trump is a racist" narrative, and it dispels the myth that Hispanics are overwhelmingly soft on migration issues.

Speaking of Fox News, I returned to the network and signed as a contributor after Trump won. With Trump in the White House, all the networks suddenly searched for Trump voices, but there were just not many credible, TV-trained advocates to go around! Talking heads for the GOP establishment abounded and still do. But pundits who are not only talented at TV but also committed to the populist Right agenda? We were in very short supply back in 2017 when Trump was inaugurated. We still are today, unfortunately. Throw in "Hispanic" to that biography mix, and you are now talking a very, very short bench.

How many Hispanics believe fully in America First principles and can handle the fire of hostile live interviews? After the name "Steve Cortes," it's not a long list. More details in the conclusion to this book on how we change that dearth and create more credible voices.

So, I spent 2017 at Fox News, trying to fully juggle my politics and media work with a full-time Wall Street gig as chief strategist for a major international brokerage. It was a lot, but at least the media side of my work was mostly easy compared to the daily verbal combat of the 2016 election season.

But the respite of working with sane people at Fox News was merely the calm before the storm, as President Trump soon asked me to move over to CNN as his Hispanic America First voice in primetime among the opposition media. I actually welcomed the challenge, especially because of the international reach of CNN. It was, and is, the only American network with real influence all over the world. In fact, much of the globe, especially decision-makers overseas, think CNN simply is the United States.

I was very aware of this international reach because of my business career, which frequently took me to London, Paris, Amsterdam, and Geneva. The decision-makers of finance all watched CNN, which explains why they were so unreasonably scared about Trump's victory in 2016. So, I hoped to be a voice on that channel to portray the facts of the America First movement to the rest of the world. To some small degree, I succeeded. For example, I heard from many influential non-Americans that they appreciated my advocacy for an America First foreign policy that sought peace and a non-interventionist agenda of realism and restraint abroad. After years of warfare all over the world, the endless interventionism of the Washington War Machine was awful for America, costing our nation dearly in blood and treasure, but it was also terrible for the rest of the world, including the hundreds of thousands of Middle Easterners killed by Bush and Obama's constant warfare there.

But on the whole, my experiences at CNN were not productive in terms of serious discussions of the patriotic populist Right. I tried mightily, but the biased anchors and shouting matches mostly precluded serious analysis and discussions. I appreciate that CNN brought me onboard and attempted to provide some semblance of balance to its programming, but the reality of super-biased producers and anchors made the task nearly impossible.

Still, the experience sharpened my media skills. Every night I was walking into the verbal octagon. I was sometimes given a guide that was different from everyone else's. Their emails would have the correct information about the topics to be discussed or media elements to be used during an appearance, but mine would be incorrect.

Of course, most nights I could figure out what we were actually discussing, and it usually flowed from the early script of *Morning Joe*. To this day, I watch at least part of the a.m. show on MSNBC. Why? Not because it's remotely interesting, engaging, or even sane, but because the lazy producers of mainstream media largely just take the script of *Morning Joe* and run it all day and into the evening. For real. So I was normally prepared for my CNN hits, even if I had not been correctly informed about other guests, topics, and so forth.

My CNN tenure ended ignobly, as one might expect. I was on-air nearly every day in 2018 and the first half of 2019. I was then suddenly completely removed. The reason? I filmed a five-minute video for PragerU, run by my friend, national radio host Dennis Prager.[85] I was a frequent guest on his radio show, and he was very impressed about my extensive work in opinion pieces and radio appearances debunking the ridiculous Charlottesville "Fine People Hoax."

So, we did a video where I used the actual transcript of what Trump said in that infamous Charlottesville reaction press conference, and I exposed the pernicious media lie that persists to this very day. President Trump never praised bigots; in fact, he explicitly denounced them in no uncertain language.

The reference to "very fine people" was clearly about the removal of the Robert E. Lee statue from the park in Charlottesville; it was not equivocating about neo-Nazis. Here are Trump's clear words from that day:

> Excuse me, they didn't put themselves down as neo-Nazis, and you had some very bad people in that group. But you also had people that were very fine people on both sides. You had people in that group—excuse me, excuse me—I saw the same pictures you did. You had people in that group that were there to protest the taking down of, to them, a very, very important statue and the renaming of a park from Robert E. Lee to another name.[86]

---

85 Steve Cortes, "What Happened in Charlottesville?" (PragerU, August 5, 2019), https://www.prageru.com/video/what-happened-in-charlottesville.

86 Donald Trump, "Read the complete transcript of President Trump's remarks at Trump Tower on Charlottesville" (*Los Angeles Times,* August 15, 2017), https://www.latimes.com/politics/la-na-pol-trump-charlottesville-transcript-20170815-story.html.

After another question at that press conference, Trump became even more explicit: "I'm not talking about the neo-Nazis and white nationalists, because they should be condemned totally."[87]

I wrote about this controversy in March 2019:

> As a man charged with publicly explaining Donald Trump's often meandering and colloquial vernacular in highly adversarial TV settings, I appreciate more than most the sometimes-murky nature of his off script commentaries. But these Charlottesville statements leave little room for interpretation. For any honest person, therefore, to conclude that the president somehow praised the very people he actually derided, reveals a blatant and blinding level of bias. Nonetheless, countless so-called journalists have furthered this damnable lie.[88]

I also tried to correct the lie whenever it came up at CNN in my frequent TV appearances, but the other guests and anchors would simply repeat the lie and claim I was mistaken. So I made the PragerU video, which was then posted on Twitter by President Trump and earned an astounding eight million views in short order. I was allowed to do the video per my contract, which gave CNN television exclusivity only, but their executives were enraged by my appearance. The video also makes no reference

---

[87] Ibid.

[88] Steve Cortes, "Trump Didn't Call Neo-Nazis 'Fine People.' Here's Proof" (*Real Clear Politics*, March 21, 2019), https://www.realclearpolitics.com/articles/2019/03/21/trump_didnt_call_neo-nazis_fine_people_heres_proof_139815.html.

to CNN at all; I very deliberately did not criticize my employer. Nonetheless, they took me off the air while also refusing to let me out of my contract.[89] They literally paid me to not work. Now, some folks out there may think such a situation is quite a deal! Maybe it is for a week or two, but I wanted to be in the arena fighting for this country...not paid to be taken off the field!

Think of the level of antipathy it takes toward our movement for a major news organization to pay a commentator to stay quiet.

This situation reveals the extreme brokenness of the corporate media and the intense level of systemic bias. In their minds, my Hispanic heritage made the situation even worse, because I was (and am) harder to dismiss as some supposedly racist, America First, white guy reactionary.

Here is one of the main takeaways from my media experience and analysis about the present and future of the American press: If I am right about Hispanics being indispensable for reclaiming our republic, then we need new and better Hispanic media resources going forward—both on-air talent and news platforms. More on those tasks in the concluding chapter.

89 Asawin Suebsaeng and Maxwell Tani, "'Where's Steve?': Trump Frets as CNN Benches His Biggest Defender" (Daily Beast, August 21, 2019), https://www.thedailybeast.com/trump-frets-over-benching-of-his-biggest-defender-on-cnn-wheres-steve-cortes.

FAITH, PRO-LIFE, CHRISTIANITY

This book's title obviously points toward men, the bad hombres who rally to the political Right and the movement of patriotic populism. Indeed, that trend is more pronounced, so far, among Latino men instead of women. But make no mistake, there are also legions of "bad mujeres"—Latina women who see things similarly and act as political trendsetters, ushering in a new era of Hispanics as a key right-wing constituency.

One such amazing woman who I consider a female version of a bad hombre is Lourdes Aguirre, an influential political activist and leader of the pro-life movement.

More on Lourdes shortly, but first let us consider the broader backdrop of the pro-life cause, Hispanics, and the political possibilities therein.

Debating the morality of the status of the unborn nearly always leads to discussions about faith, specifically Christianity. Calling America a Christian nation has become a bit of a public skirmish in recent decades. To some degree, that label represents a diversionary designation. It is a matter of historical fact that the United States was settled and founded by an overwhelmingly Christian population. Additionally, the Founding Fathers were clearly motivated by the Judeo-Christian principles of Western Civilization.

But of course, those same Founders made certain to preclude the establishment of an official state church of any religion or denomination. For the first two centuries of America's existence, this arrangement worked incredibly well. Our land was populated by practicing Christians who sustained a prevailing culture that more or less aligned with church mores and norms. All the while, religious tolerance was expected and enforced, ensuring freedom of conscience for those who choose to reject Christianity or religion itself.

But nonetheless, citizens motivated and animated by faith undergirded the American republic and supported domestic tranquility with some very notable exceptions of internal strife. After all, Thomas Jefferson himself, who is often cited by contemporary leftists as their favorite Founding Father, praised the faith of Americans in his Inaugural Address of 1801. He characterized the citizenry as "enlightened by a benign religion, professed, indeed, and practiced in various forms, yet all of them inculcating honesty, truth, temperance, gratitude, and the love of man." Similarly, his rival and predecessor as president, John Adams, observed: "Our constitution was made only for a moral and religious people. It is wholly inadequate to the government of any other."

Clearly, things have changed dramatically over the centuries and especially in recent decades, as America gravitates to a much less Christian, more agnostic culture. Right now, the fastest-growing "religion" in America is the "nones"—those who profess no faith and do not belong to any religious congregation at all.

In fact, for the first time in US history, a majority of citizens do not belong to any house of worship, as reported by a 2021 Gallup poll.[90] This survey showed that only 47 percent of Americans claim membership, down from 70 percent as recently as 1999. Gallup first measured membership in houses of worship in the 1930s, and that recorded percentage stayed at 70 or higher for six decades until this recent plunge.

So…is America still a Christian nation, or at least one animated by Christian principles? The only rational, honest answer from the data is no. As an aside, I happen to believe that the only real, lasting renaissance of American society must involve a spiritual rebirth—a new Great Awakening that is guided by the Holy Spirit. But for the purposes of this book and the strategies of the America First movement, my emphasis here remains on the secular realms of politics and policy.

Given the significant declines in Christian adherence and broad religious participation in America, what are some of the societal ramifications? Perhaps nowhere is the secularization trend more apparent than in family structure.

Back in the early 1960s, well before widespread abortion was legal in the United States, only 7 percent of all children were born to unwed mothers. Clearly the combination of religious belief plus a social stigma against unmarried mothers made single moms a rarity. Today, the opposite situation prevails, as the void of religious boundaries around premarital and extramarital sex produces a culture that celebrates promiscuity. As such, the out of wedlock birth rate is now a stunning six times higher than two

---

90 Bryan Walsh, "America is losing its religion" (Axios, April 7, 2021), https://www.axios.com/2021/04/07/americans-less-religious-gallup-poll.

generations ago, resulting in well over 40 percent of new babies entering the world without married parents.[91]

Looking at that data on unwed births by race provides an even more stark reality about how massively our society has changed as it de-Christianized. In 1965, the black unwed birth rate was 24 percent and considered a national crisis.[92] At that time, the white unwed birth rate was only 3 percent. Today, the white unwed birth rate has soared ninefold and now stands at 28 percent, well above the level that was considered shocking for blacks in 1960s America.[93] The black rate has risen to a supermajority of births at 70 percent.[94]

These numbers are even more shocking given the massive growth in abortions. In the post-Roe era, with abortions terminating over 1 million babies per year, undoubtedly the out-of-wedlock numbers would be far higher, still, if those unborn babies were allowed to live.

This point of this analysis is not at all to demonize women who find themselves in unplanned pregnancies. In fact, all human life must be cherished and welcomed as an incredible gift, even when the circumstances are not ideal, such as outside of a loving, stable marriage. Rather, these statistics on the trend of family structure speak to something much deeper about the foundations

---

91 Robert VerBruggen, "How We Ended Up With 40 Percent of Children Born Out of Wedlock" (Institute for Family Studies, December 18, 2017), https://ifstudies.org/blog/how-we-ended-up-with-40-percent-of-children-born-out-of-wedlock.

92 George A. Akerlof and Janet L. Yellen, "An analysis of out-of-wedlock births in the United States" (Brookings Institution, August 1, 1996), https://www.brookings.edu/articles/an-analysis-of-out-of-wedlock-births-in-the-united-states/.

93 Roger Clegg, "Percentage of Births to Unmarried Women" (*National Review*, February 10, 2020), https://www.nationalreview.com/corner/percentage-of-births-to-unmarried-women/.

94 Ibid.

of our society. The net result of a secular America has been most deleterious.

As America becomes less broadly religious and less specifically Christian, social pathologies rise apace. How, then, can this trend be arrested? Can it be at least slowed, if not actually reversed?

Here, Hispanics may well present the very solution American needs. Why? Because, looking at those societal trends, it seems clear that the growing influence of Hispanics can transform and potentially reverse America's lurch toward secularism.

Admittedly, Hispanics themselves are not nearly as connected to Christianity as in past decades. Though Hispanic assimilation mostly represents a welcome phenomenon for America, this is not the case with regards to the rise of secularization. Nonetheless, the evidence and data reveal that Hispanics in the United States remain decidedly more devout and attached to faith than the rest of the US population.

Here are some of the numbers. As mentioned above, America broadly has morphed into a nation of agnosticism, where the majority does not claim membership in any house of worship at all. The percentage of religious "nones" among Hispanics has similarly been rising, but it does so less quickly, and it originates from a far lower baseline. According to Pew Research Center, the current share of Hispanics who claim no religious affiliation stands at 23 percent—less than half the overall percentage for 2020s America.[95]

Perhaps even more important than membership or affiliation with a house of worship, however, is that only 3 percent of

---

[95] Russell Contreras, "Latino atheists, non-religious grow" (Axios, August 25, 2022), https://www.axios.com/2022/08/25/latino-religious-nones-surge-atheists-agnostics

Hispanics are God-denying atheists.[96] Though the Hispanics number has risen from a paltry 1 percent of atheism in 2009, it still stands far below the overall American average at 19 percent who do not believe in any God.[97] Alarmingly, that rise in American unbelievers recently doubled, after trending at a stable rate around 10 percent for many decades, according to Gallup polling from the 1940s through the beginning of this century.[98]

Even within Christianity itself, the differences between Hispanics and non-Hispanic Americans stand out starkly. For example, fully 77 percent of Hispanics in America identify as Christians.[99] Roughly half are Catholics and one-fifth are Evangelicals, with the latter group growing rapidly in recent years both here and in Latin America.

Notably, only 5 percent of Hispanics belong to mainline Protestant denominations in America. Hispanics are indeed a rarity in the Episcopal, Presbyterian, and Methodist churches that formerly dominated religious and public life in America. This reality speaks volumes and points to the far greater religious fervor of Hispanics in America and the far greater potential, therefore, for Hispanics to become a transformative force in reclaiming America as a republic based in conservative culture.

Specifically, those establishment Protestant denominations slide into cultural and political irrelevance as those churches largely neutered into ineffective social clubs masquerading as

96 Ibid.

97 Erin Doherty, "America's belief in God hits new low" (Axios, June 17, 2022), https://www.axios.com/2022/06/17/belief-god-low-gallup-poll.

98 Jeffrey M. Jones, "Belief in God in U.S. Dips to 81%, a New Low," Gallup, June 17, 2022, news.gallup.com/poll/393737/belief-god-dips-new-low.aspx.

99 "Religious Landscape Study: Latinos" (Pew Research Center) https://www.pewresearch.org/religious-landscape-study/database/racial-and-ethnic-composition/latino/. Accessed June 13, 2024.

churches. Many, if not most, of those mainline congregations now cease to operate as real Gospel churches. Not surprisingly, few new adherents are drawn to such neutrality and moral ambiguity.

Therefore, the mainline churches miss out on attracting the largest, fastest-growing, new ethnic group in America. As a consequence, the raw numbers and overall cultural influence of the mainline churches slouch as most of those pulpits increasingly promote feel good, ahistorical versions of watered-down Christianity at best, and aggressive secular humanism and Marxism at worst.

Thankfully, Hispanics have overwhelmingly rejected such milquetoast imitations of modern Christianity, and they instead gravitate to the far more rigorous and authentic reflections of Gospel truth to be found in Catholic and Evangelical doctrines. So Hispanics overall represent a far more God-fearing population on the whole, as reported by the research. But, even more importantly, within the realm of self-identified believers, Hispanics fully immerse themselves in far more demanding and scrupulous faith traditions.

The pro-life issue reflects the greater religious fervor and more devout Christianity of Hispanics in America. For example, a Pew Research Center survey in 2018 reported that 61 percent of white Americans believe that abortion should be legal in most/all cases, but only 44 percent of Hispanics concur.[100] A more recent 2022 showed the gap between the Hispanic pro-life stance and the rest of the population has shrunk, but it also confirmed that

---

[100] Steve Cortes, "Hispanics Rally to Trump, Boosting is 2020 Chances" (*Real Clear Politics*, April 2, 2019), https://www.realclearpolitics.com/articles/2019/04/02/hispanics_rally_to_trump_boosting_his_2020_chances_139933.html.

Hispanics remain more pro-life than the country as a whole.[101] The 2022 poll also confirmed that the quickly expanding Hispanic evangelical community remains decidedly pro-life, with a stunning 69 percent reporting that abortion should be illegal most/all of the time.[102]

As such, Hispanics form a growing and giant cadre of presently or potentially pro-life allies for the patriotic populist movement, subscribing to cultural conservatism and wanting to build a culture of life. When analyzing this polarizing and contentious political and cultural issue, intentionally pro-family Hispanics stand ready to convert America on the sanctity of unborn life. Hispanics are natural allies with the social conservative Right, given that Latinos are already more pro-life and more Christian than the rest of America. Moreover, as discussed, they are not just nominally Christian, but far more dedicated to demanding lives of faith as Catholics and Evangelicals.

This pro-life willingness on the part of Hispanics explains, at least in part, why they gravitate to the Republican Party generally and to patriotic populist candidates specifically. Other parts of this book detail the amazing share of Hispanic votes earned in Florida by Governor Ron DeSantis for his reelection campaign in 2022. His swing in Miami-Dade County alone was an astounding 31 percent net gain from 2018 to 2022. In his first narrow win, DeSantis got clobbered in the urban, highly Hispanic Miami-Dade by 21 percent. But four years later, his romp to reelection was propelled, in large part, by his massive rally in Miami-Dade,

---

101 Jens Manuel Krogstad, Khadijah Edwards, and Mark Hugo Lopez, "Hispanics' views on key issues facing the nation" (Pew Research Center, September 29, 2022), https://www.pewresearch.org/2022/09/29/hispanics-views-on-key-issues-facing-the-nation/.

102 Ibid.

where he triumphed by 10 percent for a net 31 percent swing in only four years.

Numerous factors drove that incredible surge in favor of DeSantis, but most pronounced was the movement in the majority-Hispanic areas of South Florida, and not just among the traditionally Republican, Cuban population around Miami. Instead, DeSantis saw massive gains among Floridians of Colombian, Puerto Rican, and Venezuelan heritage. This increase for DeSantis speaks to the willingness of Hispanics to support a thoroughly pro-life leader. DeSantis has always been clear and resolute in his insistence that we protect the lives of precious unborn babies and care for women in difficult situations with unplanned pregnancies.

In fact, shortly after his reelection, DeSantis was able to sign pro-life legislation in Florida that protects the unborn in the Sunshine State. Of course, that life-affirming legislation was only made possible because of the historic Dobbs decision, which overturned the illogical and overreaching Roe v. Wade decision.

But the Dobbs decision was only possible because of Florida. Why? Because Florida and its twenty-nine electoral votes in 2016 formed a key pillar of the stunning Donald Trump victory over Hillary Clinton. It was perhaps the greatest upset in all of US political history, and it was made possible by Hispanics all over America, especially in key swing states like Florida. That victory, in turn, allowed for President Trump to follow through on his promises to appoint federal judges and Supreme Court justices who respect the Constitution and take a restrained approach to jurisprudence, rather than individuals who take a leftist activist angle from the bench.

On Roe v. Wade specifically, the justices of the Supreme Court clearly inserted themselves into a contentious political debate, and they simply invented a Constitutional right that did not exist, neither in the actual text nor in court precedence. The justices wanted abortion legal everywhere and at nearly all times, and they effectively legislated as such from the bench. Roe deprived the American people of the right to determine when life begins and what guardrails and restrictions should be placed upon medical termination of pregnancies in the womb. This decision process on such a fundamental question of life and public morality should, of course, be determined through deliberative democratic processes. Instead, the leftist potentate justices robbed the people of their agency and issued dictates from on high.

But, after decades of prayer and political activism, that decision-making power was rightly returned to the people. The Dobbs decision only unfolded because of dedicated prayer and political warriors across America who advocated for a pro-life agenda and child-protecting candidates like Ron DeSantis and Donald Trump.

Hispanics formed a key part of this pro-family coalition, as it was a natural extension of the pro-life and observantly Christian character of the Hispanic community in America. One such warrior is Lourdes Aguirre in Florida. I first met Lourdes during the Trump 2016 campaign. She was a firecracker organizer and campaigner for Trump and the America First movement. Lourdes' reach extended throughout America, but her most profound results were found in her home state, which she crisscrossed tirelessly as an advocate and surrogate, both for in-person events and media hits.

Her activism was even more impressive given the incredibly busy life she lead outside of her political engagement. Lourdes is a mother of four beautiful daughters, and one was still young and at home during that campaign. As a widow and single mom, Lourdes carried out the duties of a loving parent alone. In addition, she was (and still is) a very successful entrepreneur in real estate, with all the responsibilities of a business owner with a thriving enterprise that took her all over the state.

Despite this packed schedule, Lourdes found the time and energy to traverse Florida advocating for conservative principles, especially the pro-life message. In churches and pregnancy centers, Lourdes made the case to convince mothers and fathers to be welcome to new life, even when the new baby arrives as a surprise. Moreover, Lourdes provided the logical, scientific case for why unborn babies should be protected by law.

In total, during that 2016 cycle, with hundreds of appearances and speaking engagements at churches, community centers, and GOP gatherings, Lourdes earned a stunning amount of new voter registrations that designated themselves as Republican voters. Her running total was over five thousand new voters. As someone who is deeply involved in campaigns and receives constant information about field organizing, I can report, that total is simply incredible. It would be an impressive sum for an entire team, not just one person. That success speaks to the dedication, hustle, and winning charisma of Lourdes, though she would surely ascribe the success to the Holy Spirit acting through her.

The political reality is that this combination of human agency and divine inspiration produced a groundswell of new support for the movement in Florida, and much of it emanates from the Latino community. Of course, Lourdes and others like her did not retire after 2016 to bask in that incredible success. The trend toward the Right, in fact, accelerated in Florida after 2016, and especially during the hugely successful first term of Ron DeSantis as governor. From 2018 to 2022, 596,000 new Republican voters registered in Florida, compared to a paltry 27,000 new Democrats.[103] That nearly 20–1 political tidal wave in favor of the GOP has shifted Florida from a crucial swing state to a decidedly red one in only the span of a few years.

A huge factor in that shift was Hispanics, and a big driver of winning over those Hispanics flowed from convincing and authentic voices like Lourdes Aguirre. In recognition of her efforts and her skills, Lourdes and I were named by President Trump as commissioners to the White House Commission on Hispanic Prosperity. This official White House working group was created to find ways to enhance and accelerate the upward mobility of Hispanic citizens in America. To be clear, the same policies that work to help Hispanics help themselves also work for working-class Americans of every ethnicity and color. We on the populist Right must never fall into the seductive leftist trap of viewing people principally through the lens of immutable characteristics.

Instead, we see all citizens as treasured Americans, whether they boast a heritage that extends back to the Mayflower, or the Spanish at St. Augustine, Florida, or even if they were legally naturalized as citizens last week. Moreover, working-class citizens of all backgrounds share many of the same hurdles and the same aspirations, so the policies that Aguirre and I promoted on the White House Commission, while marketed toward Hispanics, in reality produce a compelling agenda for all working-class Americans, whether they are brown, white, black, or purple.

---

[103] Nick Reynolds, "Republicans Gained 20 Times More Voters Than Dems in Florida in Four Years" (*Newsweek*, October 26, 2022), https://www.newsweek.com/florida-republicans-gain-more-new-voters-that-democrats-since-2018-1754664.

On that White House panel, I learned so much more about Lourdes and her amazing American story. She was born in Cuba in 1962 just as dictator Fidel Castro consolidated power. As a girl, her family sent her to America in 1970 to escape the abuses and oppression of Castro's communist regime. Aguirre was welcomed by parishioners in California. She attended an all-girls Catholic high school where the devoted nuns instilled in her a respect for unborn children. In those days in the 1970s, as legal abortion began to spread across America and become commonplace, the Catholic Church formed almost the only opposition to the new trend and the permissive laws. It took years for Evangelicals to powerfully arrive and also join in the fight for life.

Though Lourdes now worships in non-Catholic churches, she credits those nuns with giving her an appreciation for mothers and children, including the unborn. Lourdes told me those lessons were ingrained in her heart.

Throughout her life, she has passed on this same fire to love and preserve human life and to protect families. Once she moved to Florida and became more politically active, this message went from personal to public.

As a mother of four and grandmother of nine (and counting), Lourdes Aguirre speaks with love, compassion, and power about the wonders of family, even when circumstances are difficult. When she provides her persuasive witness to reasonable people, they nearly always soften their hearts on the issues of life. Many, if not most, of those same people then translate their heart change into political action, joining our movement as supporters and reliable voters. This shift is especially true among Hispanic Americans, as demonstrated by the countless examples of statistical evidence this book provides.

Lourdes reports that Hispanics are particularly welcoming to the pro-family message of the pro-life cause because Hispanics value multi-generational family structures. She points out, for example, how many multi-generational households she knows among her own relatives and Hispanic friends. Lourdes noted that Hispanics consider it a sacred responsibility to care for family members nearing the end of life. That concern for the vulnerable who are aged naturally also extends to the vulnerable who are so young. This is not just an assumed stereotype about Hispanics, but data points confirm this cultural trait. For example, Hispanic households are statistically larger than non-Hispanic ones in America. In addition, AP polling shows that Hispanics report being much more willing to care for elderly relatives than non-Hispanics.[104]

But, as powerful as the pro-life and pro-family Hispanic statistics are, the voting numbers flow from the flesh-and-blood work of political missionaries working in the field, so to speak. This is accomplished by people like Lourdes Aguirre, for example, who possess the credibility and passion to stir hearts, move minds, and change political dynamics. In the case of her efforts and the overall trajectory of Florida politically, it is difficult to overstate just how important this change is for the country as whole.

Florida proved during the draconian lockdowns of COVID-19 that it now functions as a key refuge for all America. Places like New York, Illinois, and California threw aside logic, common sense, science, and the rule of law to institute harsh crackdown measures to intimidate and control people under the fake guise of protecting health. In reality, tyrannical governors like Cuomo,

---

[104] Cary Funk and Mark Hugo Lopez, "A brief statistical portrait of U.S. Hispanics" (Pew Research Center, June 14, 2022), https://www.pewresearch.org/science/2022/06/14/a-brief-statistical-portrait-of-u-s-hispanics/.

Pritzker, and Newsom merely used the pretense of public health to gain dictatorial control over society. They punished small businesses, closed churches, and put small children into cruel, compulsory face coverings.

Thankfully, Florida provided an escape valve. It became a place of reason and science where hundreds of thousands were able to flee the abuses of Mayors de Blasio and Lori Lightfoot for the land of Ron DeSantis and his amazing top medical advisor, Dr. Joseph Ladapo. Even for those who could not relocate or chose to stay in harsh jurisdictions for personal or work reasons, the Florida model proved crucial in showing America how to safely and aggressively reopen.

Now, on the issue of abortion, Florida once again becomes the "lead blocker," to use football terminology. Just as with COVID-19 mitigation and containment, here too, real science argues persuasively on the side of respecting life in the womb. The science, put bluntly, gets more pro-life every day. Why? Because the independent viability of the unborn child trends earlier and earlier in pregnancy as medical technology advances. In addition, new research proves further the reality of the child's separate and unique genetic makeup from the beginning of pregnancy.

Thanks to Florida, we can have these crucial discussions and engage in this necessary debate the correct way. The definition of human life and the responsible restrictions of pregnancy termination are foundational societal decisions and should have never been the purview of seven men on the Supreme Court a half century ago. Florida both paved the way to overturn the injustice of Roe and now also takes the lead in protecting life. This opportunity arises largely because of Hispanics, who played such a pivotal role in the elections of both President Trump and Governor DeSantis.

Now, as the initially Washington-focused pro-life battle turns into fifty individual state efforts to win hearts and minds over to cherish life, Hispanics will form the vanguard of the new, diffused movement. In particular, Hispanic Evangelical churches will prove pivotal in this effort. Mind you, this great task is not merely about laws. The statutes we pass through the legislative process of a democratic republic are important, of course. Moreover, those laws often do shape culture. Many political operatives get hung up on the debate about whether politics is downstream of culture, or vice versa. The only correct answer to that either/or question is yes. It is a mixture and often changing; both politics and culture are intertwined, and determining which one is in the lead or forms the other is really an irrelevant task because they are too codependent to be separated anyway.

Even accepting that philosophical reality, it is clear that the pro-family, pro-child movement in America cannot merely focus on changing laws. After a full half century of the madness and sadness of Roe, we must also sway individual perspectives and begin the long march of changing the culture. It took two generations for abortion on demand, for any reason, and at any point of pregnancy to become a tragic norm in American society. The political and cultural reality is that it will undoubtedly take years, perhaps decades, to form a societal consciousness that affirms life in all its stages, including that of the vulnerable unborn child.

For this reason, and considering this pivotal 2024 election in terms of practical politics, pro-life activists and voters need to acknowledge two important realities. First, federalism works, even when we do not appreciate the results of pushing power to states and localities. Determining crucial, foundational questions of our humanity should be the task of governments that are closest to the people. Existential questions like: When does human life begin? or What constitutes a marriage? must and should be left to the states. This delegation is not an abdication and, again, Hispanics have a vital new role in America to serve as persuasive champions for family, children, and the dignity of all human life.

Second, Hispanic Christians should be at the forefront of a pro-life movement that shifts its focus to achieve political as well as cultural success for the cause. Whenever we on the Right get caught up in talking about restrictions and obsessing over timeline limits within pregnancy, we can easily fall into the debates that the anti-child, secular humanist Left wants us to have regarding abortion. In fact, these "debates" are rarely real discussions and instead devolve into shouting matches of two groups of totally contradictory worldviews simply talking past each other.

As such, in order to engage in a real discussion, particularly at the federal level, we must initiate a proactive agenda to encourage as many women as possible to choose life and create the tangible assistance those women need to make that affirmative choice.

Now, am I being politically naive? Can the abortion issue actually be transformed into a political positive for conservatives and pro-lifers into the November 2024 elections, all the while helping women and saving babies?

The answer is yes!

But candidates and leaders must avoid the media traps and instead embrace a fresh vision that boldly emphasizes an America First baby boom, providing real support for women to choose life.

Regarding the federalism that so far prevails since the Dobbs decision, a constitutional, 10th Amendment-appropriate process has worked. In states like New York and Illinois, nothing has changed regarding the laws that permit abortion. But in red states like Texas and Tennessee, abortion numbers have plunged or even disappeared.

These wins in red states are momentous, and we should all give thanks. But the issue is hardly settled on a national basis, and it could play a destructive role for the Right into the 2024 general election. We need to be clear-eyed about this reality from the presidency down to local campaigns. Conventional wisdom indicates that most, or all, of the potential political peril faces pro-life Republican candidates.

But in reality, the radicalism of the Democratic Party also presents political risk to pro-abortion candidates, especially if the pro-life movement can coalesce around natalist America First strategies that promote family growth, American children, and support and encouragement for pregnant mothers.

So, what are those strategies?

First, we must frame this issue correctly. We in the pro-life movement should not limit ourselves to gestational protections for unborn babies. Current international laws and polling data confirm a strong consensus among civilized people for rules against late-term abortions and procedures that inflict excruciating pain upon a baby in the womb.

But the conversation should not stop at proposals for regulations and limits; it should also emphasize the need for government policy to actively help more mothers make the choice to keep their children. The Left, for example, has successfully used taxpayer money at every level of government to promote the pro-abortion agenda with alarming effectiveness. It's high time our side similarly harnesses government resources to help vulnerable moms, while actively promoting a necessary and hopeful America First baby boom.

Such a shift would put the Left on the defensive. After all, the pro-abortion fringe has become so radicalized that it will not accept any limits on abortion. Long-gone is the Bill Clinton idea of abortion that is safe, legal, and rare. Instead, the era of Joe Biden and Kamala Harris insists on abortions that are celebrated, taxpayer-funded, and unrestrained.

That Biden-Harris radicalism carries political risk for the Democrats. For instance, among Michigan Catholics, 52 percent consider the Democrats too extreme on abortion, and only 36 percent consider them mainstream on abortion.[105] Such a spread in a key battleground state points to election risks for Democrats as well; this is particularly so because the Catholic vote has historically been determinative.[106] Catholics split almost exactly evenly in the 2020 election but had increased by 8 percent for Trump when he won in 2016.[107] In fact, for a half century prior to 2020, Catholic voters determined the presidential winner in every election except for the year 2000.

But Republicans cannot only assail the anti-life extremism of the Democrats. After enduring decades of on-demand abortions that are mandated by the high court, rebuilding a culture of life in America will require a generational effort. In this politically polarized national environment, the possibility of congressional

---

[105] Jon McHenry and Dan Judy, "Key Findings from Survey of Michigan Likely Voters" (*North Star Opinion Research*, February 26, 2024), https://www.amworkers.com/news.

[106] Domenico Montanaro, "The myth of the Catholic swing vote" (PBS News Hour, March 27, 2014), https://www.pbs.org/newshour/politics/myth-catholic-swing-vote.

[107] Ruth Igielnik, Scott Keeter, and Hannah Hartig, "Behind Biden's 2020 Victory" (Pew Research Center, June 30, 2021), https://www.pewresearch.org/politics/2021/06/30/behind-bidens-2020-victory/.

action on any national abortion ban is next to zero. We must be honest about this reality on Capitol Hill. Congress is far from enacting national pro-life legislation; in fact, it is far more likely to codify the madness of Roe if we do not play our political cards correctly in 2024. The idea of a Biden win and a GOP sweep of the House is not remotely out of the question. I do not believe such an outcome is likely, and I am confident that both Trump and other America First, pro-family candidates will win, but such victories are hardly assured in a nation as polarized as America in the 2020s.

Therefore, we in the pro-life movement and on the political Right should prioritize a government-wide agenda that invests, subsidizes, protects, and promotes pregnant mothers' decision to choose life. Such an agenda would drive Hispanic support, particularly among Latina women.

Research suggests that substantial numbers of women would, in fact, choose life with better financial and personal support. For instance, a peer-reviewed study from the pro-life Charles Lozier Institute, posted by the NIH, found that among women who aborted, "sixty percent reported they would have preferred to give birth if they had received more support from others or had more financial security."[108]

A new baby boom must provide federal resources to help that majority make that choice for life, even if they live in places of unfettered abortion like California. Generous financial support for pregnant women and new mothers makes sense. Better, longer maternal leave statutes should also be passed along with

[108] David C. Readon, Katherine A. Rafferty, and Tessa Longbons, "The Effects of Abortion Decision Rightness and Decision Type on Women's Satisfaction and Mental Health" (National Library of Medicine, May 11, 2023), https://www.ncbi.nlm.nih.gov/pmc/articles/PMC10257365/.

more federal resources to provide counseling, care, training, and alternatives to abortion. Federal laws should likewise prohibit coercive abortions, especially if that coercion involves taking women against their will across state lines out of pro-life jurisdictions. Further, federal policy should actively promote life affirming messages that celebrate motherhood, children, and America's growing population.

When activists masquerading as journalists try to play "gotcha" and pin down a pro-life candidate on the exact forms of restriction they are willing to support, the correct response must be to instead answer a much broader question: what can government do to help as many mothers as possible make the choice for life?

Since 2019, government reports show the abortion industry has received over $2 billion to expand and promote abortion. And these are just direct subsidies to the abortion industry itself. Imagine what a comparable investment in the pro-life movement could do. Doing so would provide real hope to pregnant mothers who today are told abortion is their only answer, while also providing candidates running for office with a rallying cry that every voter can support.

Hispanics can take the lead in the critical tasks of protecting babies and creating loving environments where all children will flourish after birth. But Republicans must be willing to eschew some of the "small government" orthodoxy that still dominates important wings of the GOP, especially at the donor level. We are $34 trillion in debt, and that number is climbing fast. Let's face the facts—the small government ship sailed long ago, even if we wish we could turn back that clock.

So instead of fixating on some fantasy of returning to a 19th century-style limited government, we need to learn lessons from the Left. Our political opponents are masterful at making the power of government work for them and form the society they want. In this case, they sadly desire a secular, brutalist society that diminishes the family and disregards children, and they have largely succeeded in this ignoble quest!

But we have the affirmative and God-ordained truth about the kind of society that flourishes—the country we all want to live in, even people who are not Christian believers. Since Hispanics have not fallen into the nihilist traps of other demographics in America, they must embrace our pivotal role in the political, cultural, and spiritual rebirth of society. Bad hombres and dedicated Latinas will rise to the occasion of this momentous task.

BAD HOMBRES—CONCLUSION

As detailed throughout this book, Hispanics now occupy a central place in the great battle to restore our nation. Even more, Hispanics must embrace the lead role in that epic cause. Can a republic founded by (mostly) Protestant whites be saved by millions of (mostly) Hispanic Catholics?

The idea may seem far-fetched at first glance, but I hope that I have made the statistical, evidence-based, logical case as to why this scenario is not just possible, but probable. Bad Hombres stand uniquely positioned to resurrect the greatness of America.

But the opposition never rests, and remains formidable, of course. In the near term, the Democratic Party becomes ever more autocratic, dishonest, and Marxist. Anyone who doubts the seriousness of the threat the 2020s Left poses to the American way of life needs to take seriously the claims of Kamala Harris and the super radical agenda she proposes.

In addition, the powerbrokers of the Democratic Party staged an unprecedented, totally backroom, underhanded bloodless coup against the rightful nominee, Joe Biden. Now, was Biden incapable of serving another term as president? Absolutely. For that matter, is he cognitively able to complete hirst first term? Clearly not.

But regardless, there are rules and principles that should—and must—govern overturning the clear will of the people in selecting the party's nominee through a primary process. Instead, Kamala Harris was simply selected, not elected, by the oligarchs of the Democrats, including mega donors, Nancy Pelosi, and Chuck Schumer. Such "smoke filled room" politics stink and clearly disenfranchise millions of voters.

But even more importantly, these dirty maneuvers once again expose the treachery and vast control of the oligarchs and the American ruling class. In the momentous struggle to topple that crooked system, Hispanics are absolutely essential. We have the scale—meaning the masses of bodies—plus the community characteristics to politically punch back against this kind of cronyism to reclaim the American republic.

In some ways, Hispanics are particularly suited for this task because of the corruption and pervasive Marxism that have so afflicted Latin America, our ancestral home. For example, when Kamala Harris proposes price controls on food, Hispanic citizens of America who hail from places like Cuba and Venezuela cry out in opposition immediately, knowing all too well that such Marxist measures lead to shortages, black markets, and systemic corruption.

But rather than deal with the underlying causes of food inflation—and *all* inflation—which would mean dialing back the absolutely exorbitant level of Biden/Harris borrowing and spending, Kamala Harris simply proposes a tried-and-failed communist ploy of price controls. Bad Hombres know better. Been there, done that. We will not allow Harris and her ilk to turn America into a place of privation, to "Argentina-ize" this amazing country.

Instead, patriotic Latinos rally to the America First cause led by a successful businessman who insists that free enterprise and policy reforms return American to broad prosperity. Latinos embrace Donald Trump on the substance of such policies, as well as because of the bravery of this leader.

To the point of that bravery, all decent Americans of any political affiliation wondered at the instant strength shown by President Trump when he was shot at his rally in Pennsylvania. His immediate reaction, seconds after being shot in the head, was to pump his fist and motivate the people to "fight!" It was an incredible visual for the ages and it exemplified the perseverance of Trump the lion. That political lion persists even though he is also Trump the persecuted, enduring more unjust attacks than any other public figure in the history of America.

That reaction after the assassination attempt also points to the impressive masculinity of Trump, which rallies Hispanics to his cause in a particular way. Trump is truly the "man on horseback," but not in the repressive authoritarian way. Rather, he personifies the fortitude of a truly "bad hombre," US-version.

In this regard, Latinos will play a pivotal role not just in this 2024 election, but also in the broader struggle to rein in the globalists and reclaim the United States for the masses of patriotic, God-fearing workers of America.

That task is monumental, of course. But it is also an honor to stand tall in a crucible moment of history. How many citizens, of any country, anywhere in the world, are granted such an opportunity to engage in such a worthy cause?

While the work can seem daunting, the task is worthy and the payoffs will be generational. We are going to save America, Bad Hombres. So, let's do what we do best, and get to damn work…

ABOUT THE AUTHOR

Steve Cortes has been a cable news TV commentator for fifteen years, serving as a contributor for Fox News, CNN, and CNBC. He led Hispanic outreach for the Trump campaigns of 2016 and 2020. Prior to politics, Cortes traded global capital markets for twenty-five years on behalf of institutional investors.

www.ingramcontent.com/pod-product-compliance
Lightning Source LLC
Chambersburg PA
CBHW072246270326
41930CB00010B/2287

9781637589397